D0049967

Eating Eternity

Food, Art and Literature in France

JOHN BAXTER

Museyon

New York

Library of Congress Cataloging-in-Publication Data

Names: Baxter, John, 1939- author.
Title: Eating eternity : food, art and literature in France / John Baxter.
Description: New York : Museyon, [2017] | Includes index.
Identifiers: LCCN 2017013175 (print) | LCCN 2017014244 (ebook) | ISBN 9781938450945 (e-Pub) | ISBN 9781938450952 (e-PDF) | ISBN 9781938450969 (Mobi) | ISBN 9781940842165 (pbk.)
Subjects: LCSH: Gastronomy--France. | Dinners and dining--Social aspects--France. | Arts and society--France--History. | Artists--France--Social life and customs. | Cooking in literature.
Classification: LCC TX637 (ebook) | LCC TX637 .B39 2017 (print) | DDC 641.01/30944--dc23
LC record available at https://lccn.loc.gov/2017013175

Published in the United States and Canada by:
Museyon Inc.
1177 Avenue of the Americas, 5 Fl.
New York, NY 10036

Museyon is a registered trademark.
Visit us online at www.museyon.com
ISBN 978-1-940842-16-5

0719040

Printed in China

To Charles DeGroot and the members of that island of
lucidity, fellowship and *gourmandise*, the Paris Men's Salon.

INTRODUCTION

"Show me another pleasure like dinner which comes every day and lasts an hour."—*Charles-Maurice de Talleyrand, senior advisor to Napoleon I, Emperor of France.*

Six foreign food writers, 15 minutes late for their reservation, piled into a tiny Paris restaurant in the shadow of Hôtel des Invalides.

With a fixed professional smile, the *maîtresse d'* guided them to their table, the largest in the room. As coats were shed, seating wrangled over, enquiries made about the location of the *toilettes*, little attention was paid to the glares of other diners, some of whom, having booked months before, were paying €500 a head for what, if three Michelin stars meant anything, was some of the best food in France.

Nobody in the party took time to note the smooth leather chairs, undulating walls of pale pear wood or the glass lighting fittings by master *verrier* René Lalique, souvenired from a carriage of the original Orient Express. (The nude nymphs and shepherds molded into the glass were intended, explained the chef on his website, to evoke ancient Rome's most ecstatic ritual, the Bacchanal.)

Menus, proffered, were barely consulted, the journalists having opted for the tasting menu or *menu de dégustation:* a cruise in 12 dishes through the master chef's creations, a parade of flavors and textures designed to display his inventiveness and that of his team.

Watching from the staircase that led down to the subterranean kitchen, the chef judged the party ready to start eating, and dispatched the first course, careful to ensure that each diner received his or her plate at exactly the same moment: the so-called *service Russe* or Russian service at its most effective.

He was less pleased to see some of the journalists chatting at they ate. One even put down her fork, rummaged in her handbag for a notebook and scribbled a few lines. None commented on the food. Glaring, the chef descended into his underground domain.

Ten minutes later, waiters cleared the empty plates and served another course. As they did so, one journalist peered at his portion, then those of his colleagues.

"Didn't we just have this?"

Taking notice for the first time, the others agreed. What they'd been served was identical with what they'd just eaten.

Was this a glitch in the famously perfect service?

Were standards at France's most select restaurant starting to slip?

A waiter was summoned. A few minutes later, he returned from the kitchen.

"I spoke to the chef. And yes, he did send out the same dish twice."

"But … *why?*"

"He wants you to start the meal again. The first time, you were not paying attention."

AUTHOR'S NOTE: Portions of this book, in a different form, appeared in *The French Riviera and Its Artists* (Museyon, 2015) and in *The Perfect Meal: In Search of the Lost Tastes of France* (HarperCollins, 2013).

Eating Eternity

TABLE OF CONTENTS

Eating Eternity

TABLE OF CONTENTS

CHAPTER 1

BON APPÉTIT!

Food as cultural symbol

A mong French works of art from the early 19th century, one, a lithograph dating from 1808, holds a special interest for anyone who takes a serious interest in what we eat and drink.

Called *Les Cinq Sens* (The Five Senses), it's the work of Louis-Léopold Boilly. To illustrate all the senses in a single image, he crowds together five individuals, each signifying one of the avenues through which we perceive the world. As a girl sniffs perfume, a gentleman exercises his sense of touch by caressing her hand, while, above him, another presses his ear to a watch and, at the top of the picture, an antiquarian uses a magnifier to examine an *objet d'art*.

Les Cinq Sens (The Five Senses), Louis-Léopold Boilly, 1808

Absorbed in their private sensations, none of the four notices the fifth. Eyes wide in appreciation, he holds a plate in one hand while licking the fingers of the other. Clearly, something he's just eaten has ravished his sense of taste.

By placing a contented eater at the center of his composition, Boilly leaves us in no doubt with which of the senses his sympathies lie. Much as one would expect an artist to place greater value on the eyes, he naturally, as a Frenchman, assigned a privileged role to the palate.

In 1825, Jean Anthelme Brillat-Savarin, France's premier philosopher of cuisine, wrote in *The Physiology of Taste:* "The destiny of nations depends on how they feed themselves." To the generation that followed the fall of Napoleon in 1815, sweeping statements of this kind were not uncommon as its members searched for a new belief to motivate the continuing progress of Europe toward modernity. That food would play a part in this quest, and an important one, was a novel concept for most countries. Not so, however, for France.

For centuries, French culture was segregated into three *tiers état* or estates: the peasants and middle class or *bourgeoisie*, who made up 80 percent of the population, the *clergé* or Catholic church and the *noblesse* or nobility. (In 1787, British politicians recognized a so-called "Fourth Estate," the press).

Each estate signified its status by what it ate. The aristocracy consumed only what was noble; not of the earth. In their eyes, most vegetables, but particularly potatoes and turnips, were fit only for animals. They also ate no fruit that had touched the ground, since it was believed that such contact was poison. While an association with earth tainted the meat of cattle, sheep and pigs, animals that lived in the wild were considered edible. As with a warrior, the courage shown by a hunted and cornered animal also counted in its favor. The wild boar or *sanglier*, though a species of pig, could be hunted and eaten, since it earned nobility by living free and, when trapped, fighting savagely for survival.

The church, the ruling ritual of which replicated Christ's last meal with his disciples, regarded food as a reminder of our animal natures, to be enjoyed in moderation. Rather than rejoicing in the numerous biblical references to food, from a few baskets of bread and salt fish feeding a multitude to water becoming wine at the marriage feast at Cana, the church required believers to curtail their appetites by fasting for the 40 days of Lent and forgoing meat on Fridays.

Food was of most importance to the third estate, the peasantry, since it regulated life and death. A single failed harvest could induce famine and starvation. "The table epitomises the peasant's very existence," writes one food historian. "It is the locus of all social relations, a metonym of the earth contracted to four legs, and, when it is replete with food, an icon of the fields in which the peasant labours."

Given this history, it was inevitable that the French would excel in the appreciation of food and drink, the methods used to prepare them, the manner in which they are served, even the terms in which we discuss them. From *bouquet, bouillon, banquet, canapé, crouton, consommé, carafe, chef, entrée, gourmet* and *gastronome* to *hors d'oeuvre, menu, pâté, purée, sauce, sauté* and *terrine*, the vocabulary of cooking and eating is overwhelmingly French.

In 1927, the annual *Salon d'Automne* (Autumn Art Exhibition) officially recognized cooking as one of the fine arts, next to painting and sculpture. For a week, the best chefs in Paris took turns to prepare meals at the Salon's restaurant. By 2010, this acceptance had been internationally endorsed. In that year, UNESCO, the cultural arm of the United Nations, designated the classic French dinner or *repas* for 20 or more diners as an element in humanity's "intangible cultural heritage." To share such a meal with family and friends did more than satisfy hunger; it was "a social practice designed to celebrate the most important moments in the lives of individuals and groups."

Had anyone doubted this importance, the French language offered ample evidence. Food references pepper the slang known as *la langue verte:* the green tongue. The French equivalent of "the cat's out of the bag" is "the carrots are cooked." Someone stupid is a *navet*—a turnip—or a *poire*—a pear. Business is only discussed at the end of a meal, "between the pear and the cheese," while to behave boorishly is to "spit in the soup." It's also traditional, if a trifle old-fashioned, to wish one's fellow guests *"bon appétit"* (good appetite) as they begin a meal.

Wherever one looks in the social history of France, food is an unacknowledged subtext. Aside from those creators of the kitchen itself who, in preparing dishes for the table, do so with one eye on aesthetic appeal, the French also excel among those who paint and draw food, write about food, film and photograph food, even set it to music. Marcel Proust's cycle of 13 novels, known as *À la recherche de temps perdu* (In Search of Lost Time), hinges on the memory of a taste; that of a fragment of cake dissolved in some lime flower tea. Gérard Depardieu, one of many actors and performers to own vineyards and restaurants, also starred in a film as François Vatel, the chef who, in 1671, killed himself in the belief that the fish for a royal banquet had not arrived.

Gertrude Stein, encouraging Ernest Hemingway to refine his writing style, sent him to study the single-minded way in which Paul Cézanne painted apples. For the Surrealists of the 1920s and '30s, food was a key that unlocked secret spaces in the mind. René Magritte's *The Son of Man* shows a businessman in a bowler hat whose face is obscured by a shiny green apple. Luis Buñuel's film *Le Charme discret de la bourgeoisie* (The Discreet Charm of the Bourgeoisie) follows a group of middle-class ladies and gentleman as they drift around France, casually skirting violent death while they search for a place to eat lunch.

In the way that citizens who fail to turn out for the polls are described as "voting with their feet," the French have, occasionally, voted with their stomachs. During the 1995 presidential election, a Parisian restaurant patronized by both candidates, Jacques Chirac and Édouard Balladur, invited its clients to vote for one or the other by ordering their man's favorite dish. A preference for Chirac's hearty country sausage over the prissy Balladur's herrings in oil was reflected in the former's landslide victory.

France not only pioneered the arts of the kitchen but it was the first nation to acknowledge that certain individuals possess a unique ability to *understand* food. In defining this skill, it added another word to the

The Son of Man, René Magritte, 1964

international lexicon. A *connoisseur*, from the verb *connaître*, is someone who *knows* his subject, and whose opinion is accordingly privileged. The world of food expertise further refines the definition by distinguishing between *gourmets*, those who have a heightened appreciation of food; *gourmands* or gluttons, who carry that appreciation to excess; and *gastronomes*, defined by UNESCO as "individuals who possess deep knowledge of the [culinary] tradition and preserve its memory [and] watch over the living practice of the rites, thus contributing to their oral and/or written transmission, in particular to younger generations."

Among gastronomes, the function of food and drink is not to satisfy hunger but to tantalize, its motivation a desire, often painful in its intensity, to channel an appreciation of the world through an intentionally restricted area of the senses. Gastronomes seldom eat more than a mouthful of any dish or take more than a sip of wine. Under their influence, the best restaurants introduced a *menu de dégustation* or tasting menu, made up of a dozen or more dishes, but tiny servings of each. By removing hunger from the equation, gastronomes elevated food to the peak of discrimination. If, as the English epicurean Walter Pater suggested, all art aspires to the condition of music, then it must follow that, in France, food tends to the condition of art.

CHAPTER 2

RULES OF THE HUNT

Aristocracy's sport finds its way into art

The bubonic plague or Black Death that killed half the population of Europe between 1346 and 1353 didn't affect animals. Receding, it left vast tracts of woodland teeming with game. First for the kitchen, then for sport, landowners led packs of hounds in pursuit of wild boar, hares and deer. Trained hawks swooped on pheasants, partridge and grouse. Carp and trout were netted from freshwater streams. Chasing and killing animals offered some of the excitement of war, even

15th-century illumination of a hunting scene

a little of the danger, with the bonus that, once the hunt ended, the quarry could be turned into food that not only tasted good, but, in the manner it was served, reminded the diners of how it had been acquired. Each meal was one more moment of pleasure snatched from eternity.

To preserve the exclusivity of hunting, poaching on royal preserves was punishable by mutilation or death. Peasants who risked being blinded simply for stalking an animal were bitter that hunters could summon them at all hours to act as beaters. It was even known for noblemen who felt the cold to order serfs to defecate in a heap, then immerse their feet in the steaming pile to warm them.

The aristocracy devoted much time and effort to maintaining a countryside well-populated with creatures to hunt. "Seasons" protected animals and birds while they were mating and rearing their young. Gamekeepers raised pheasant, partridge and grouse in captivity and restocked woodland that had been "hunted out." Such dates as August 12, known in Britain as "the Glorious 12th," marking the opening of the shooting season for grouse, were red-letter days for the gentry; renewals of their license to slaughter.

Originally, all hunting was called "venery" and all meat from hunted animals classed as venison, but the definition narrowed as deer became the most popular game and their meat correspondingly valued. As "venison" came to mean only deer meat, the French coined a new word, *gibier,* to define any creature that lived free in water or the open air, and could therefore be honorably hunted.

But food was only a by-product of the hunt. The primary motive was sport, and the prey, in particular foxes, wolves or bears, often chosen for cunning and speed rather than culinary possibilities. As Oscar

Wilde scoffed at fox hunting, it was a case of "the unspeakable in pursuit of the uneatable." How one behaved during the hunt also counted for more than a successful kill. Etiquette required that the gentleman hunter not show excessive zeal or expertise, for example, by outrunning the pack or beating the hunt master to the kill. In Isabel Colegate's novel *The Shooting Party*, a lord taking part in a private shooting competition at a country house party in 1913 is exposed committing the ultimate transgression—target practice.

Hunting provided one of the few occasions in which a nobleman left home. Once gone, he was absent for the entire day, and might even stay out overnight, an opportunity for the women he left behind to explore other diversions. Venery, coined to describe hunting, acquired an additional meaning: the pursuit of sexual satisfaction. Infidelity was so common in the hunting society that a man with an unfaithful wife was signified by showing him with a pair of horns, a reference to the fact that, when a stag lost to another in combat, the winner acquired the loser's mate. The illustration to *La Double Chasse* (The Double Hunt), an 1839 poem by Pierre-Jean de Béranger, shows a hunt forming in front of a chateau. As the master and his cronies hoot on their horns, eager to be off, the lady of the house sneaks her lover through a window and some jokers slyly hang the antlers of a stag on the master's front door.

Blood was the avatar of every hunt, the symbol of a readiness to kill. The faces of boys on their first hunt were ritually smeared with blood. Medieval stories of the hunt often include the figure of the professional huntsman, a commoner ready to kill at the orders of his

Illustration to *La Double Chasse* (The Double Hunt)

master. In the traditional fable of Snow White, the queen sends such a man into the woods with orders to murder her, although, atypically, he relents. Another legend, adapted by Carl Maria von Weber for his 1821 opera *Der Freischütz* (The Free Shot), transformed the character of Samiel, the Archangel of Death who led the revolt of the angels against God, into the Black Huntsman of the Wolf's Glen, who exchanges the soul of the main character for a rifle that cannot miss.

The most vivid legend associated with hunting is that of the Wilde Jagd or Wild Hunt. Originating in Scandinavia as a hunt led by the god Odin or Woden, it took root in medieval European mythology as a manifestation of the horror that stalked the choked and overgrown woodland of the Dark Ages. Thundering over the treetops and plunging through the forest at impossible speed, the riders of the wild hunt, at the heels of a hunting pack of wolves, were thought to warn of war or plague. People in its path would be trampled, or, in some versions, whirled up in the wake of the phantom riders. In other manifestations of the myth, simply to look upon the hunt was certain death.

Having designated the hunting and eating of game as their monopoly, the gentry emphasized the fact in art. Craftsmen preserved the hide, horns, claws and heads of their kill. Skins and furs became clothing, and antlers were mounted in places of honor. Later, stuffed and mounted trophies of the hunt were supplemented by *animalier* bronzes: statuettes of game birds, hunting dogs, horses and wild boar.

Paradoxically, the first Europeans to create graphic art from the hunt were men of God. From the abbeys

Halt During the Hunt, Charles-André van Loo, 1737, Musée du Louvre

where they had preserved culture during the Dark Ages, monks of the 15th century watched as hunting parties rode out for a day's sport. Turning back to the manuscripts they were painstakingly copying and illustrating, some put aside the pious but dull images of planting and the harvest, and exercised their imagination instead with visions of pheasants exploding from the brush, hawks whirling in the air and brilliantly dressed ladies and gentlemen enjoying a few hours of sunshine and blood.

CHAPTER 3

THE FOOD OF THE POOR

Don't enquire too closely about what goes into the sausage

P aintings reveal much about the eating habits of hunters and of the farmers and servants who made their sport possible. In *The Peasant Wedding*, painted in 1567, Dutch artist Pieter Brueghel the Elder recorded a typical farmers' feast. There's no meat, fruit or fresh produce on the table, only bread, porridge and pottage: cabbage soup. Everyone drinks beer, brought to the table in earthenware jugs. Instead of plates, flat round loaves of bread called trenchers

The Peasant Wedding, Pieter Brueghel the Elder, 1567, Kunsthistorisches Museum

soaked up any spillage; a robust eater is still called a "trencherman." After the meal, the bread was thrown to the dogs: the origin of "hush puppies," the scraps of fried batter generated by modern barbecues.

For more than a century, historians believed that peasants of the Middle Ages ate almost entirely starches and carbohydrates, but recent research has modified this view. "It isn't necessarily true," writes an archaeologist, "that farmers ate only vile and formless boiled vegetables." From the analysis of middens and garbage dumps, we now know they sometimes consumed meat, eggs and fish—primarily salmon, once so common in the Thames that apprentices complained of having to eat it at every meal. Nevertheless, meat in any quantity, and particularly prime cuts, remained a luxury. The phrase "to eat meat every day" signified wealth, the equivalent of the American "gravy train."

In theory, a farmer could raise animals for food, but in practice his livestock often belonged to the landowner. Even if the farmer owned them, they were too useful to be slaughtered. The carcass of a milk cow or draught horse at the end of its productive life was generally worth only what a knacker would pay for the hide and bones to be rendered into fat and glue.

Occasionally he fattened a pig, feeding it on kitchen scraps. With no way to keep it through the winter, such animals were traditionally slaughtered on Martinmas, November 11, the feast of Saint Martin, the date by which the harvest's last grain went to store. Used sparingly, a pig could last all winter. Even a few scraps of bacon gave extra savor to

Postcard of girl with calf's head

soup, while beans simmered with sausage, a chunk of pork and a joint of preserved goose became *cassoulet*. Traditionally, housewives made this classic dish first thing in the morning, then carried it to the baker, who placed the covered ceramic pots in the oven still hot from baking the day's bread. A day of long, slow cooking conferred a particularly unctuous texture on the beans and fat meat.

This spirit of cooperation extended to the butchering of a pig, a community occasion, with the helpers paid off with a share. No part was wasted. The ears, muzzle and tail, boiled soft, chopped and added to meat from the head, were embedded in a natural jelly to make head cheese or brawn. These were traditionally served cold with sauce vinaigrette, a mixture of oil and vinegar. In a 19th-century pantomime described by Jean Cocteau, a clown loses a cooked pig's head in the ocean, but, like a cat with a saucer of milk, lures it back to land with a dish of vinaigrette. Even the blood was turned into *boudin noir* or blood sausage, for which the intestines provided casings. The last scrapings of meat and fat, mixed with cereals and spices, became dry sausages, known as *saucissons*. With salt a luxury, meat was smoked or wind-dried. Sausages joined the hams and flitches of bacon that hung in the rafters, where they accrued flavor from the smoke of cooking fires. Some *saucissons*, hard and dry as wood, could be taken on a journey. The more plump variety were boiled and served with lentils, or cold sliced potatoes (a favorite meal of Ernest Hemingway). "There are two things," folk wisdom decreed, "into the making of which one shouldn't enquire too closely—laws and sausages." One sausage, the *andouille*, later a feature of American Cajun, *i.e.*, Acadian cuisine, used the pig's intestines, including a part of the porker which, by tradition, added an authentic peppery accent; its *trou de cul* or anus.

As the most common domestic animal, the horse could have provided the peasantry with a ready source of meat, had the church not forbidden believers from eating it, citing an eighth-century ruling by Pope Gregory III that to do so was "an abomination." The Pope's objection to the eating of horseflesh was that it was practiced at the time by certain pagan tribes, but the church exploited this long-forgotten technicality to keep horse off the peasant's menu until 1870. Cooks skirted this prohibition by assuming it didn't apply to donkeys, the meat of which often found its way into *saucissons*.

CHAPTER 4

FEASTS AT VERSAILLES

Roast peacock, larks' tongues in honey and Louis XIV performs for his guests

The feast, a rare experience for the peasantry, took place daily in palaces such as Versailles. From the moment servants woke the king and queen at 7:30 a.m. with tea or hot chocolate to the time they retired about 11:30 p.m., the royal family would eat, or at least be offered two main meals, at 10 a.m. and 4 p.m., each of 20 dishes or more, as well as snacks they could slip into their pockets in case they felt peckish.

Festivity given by Louis XIV, at Versailles in 1674, feast with tables set around the fountain of the marble courtyard, Jean Le Pautre, 1676

To wash down this rich diet, the king drank only champagne, water generally being polluted, and other beverages, such as chocolate, suspect. In October 1671, Madame de Sévigné, a member of Louis's court and a tireless gossip, wrote to her pregnant daughter.

> But what do you have to say about chocolate? Are you not afraid of how it can burn the blood? What if all the effects that appear miraculous mask some sort of diabolical combustion? What do your doctors say? In your fragile state, my dear child, I need your word [that you will not drink it], because I fear that you will suffer these problems. I loved chocolate, as you know. But I think it did burn me; and furthermore, I have heard many terrible stories about it. The Marquise de Coëtlogon drank so much chocolate when she was pregnant last year that she gave birth to a baby who was black as the devil and died.

Chocolate, only recently introduced in France, via England, competed with the equally rare Chinese tea as the preferred nonalcoholic drink of the aristocracy. Initially it was credited with curative qualities, and taken as medicine. For the more familiar modern form of chocolate, as a solid, we have Marie Antoinette, the queen of Louis XVI, to thank. Disliking the taste of her morning medication, she asked her court pharmacist, Sulpice Debauve, to make it more palatable. Mixing the drug with chocolate, cane sugar and almond milk, he pressed it into coinlike discs called *pistoles,* each printed with the three gold lilies of the Bourbon monarchy— the ancestor of today's chocolate bar. One of the few

The Cup of Chocolate (The Penthièvre Family), Jean-Baptiste Charpentier, 1768, Musée de l'Histoire de France, Château de Versailles

courtiers to survive the revolution of 1789, Debauve opened a Paris shop in 1800, selling chocolate in all its forms from the same Paris premises on Rue des Saints-Pères where his descendants still do business.

A feast at one of the great *châteaux* of France during the 16th century fell somewhere between meal and show. As well as musicians who played and jesters who did tricks, the kitchen would periodically serve some elaborate creation, aimed at impressing the guests with the wealth of the host and the expertise of his cooks. These *grosses pièces* could include spit-roasted pheasant, duck, fish and, on special occasions, swan or peacock, served in their plumage. Depending on the skill of the chef, guests might also be invited to eat such *jeux d'esprit* as "meat fruit"—apples, pears and plums, convincingly molded from raw minced pork and colored to look like the real thing.

Made for display as much as to eat, the *grosses pièces* were difficult to carve, so an "esquire carver" was put in charge. This role, allocated to a favored courtier or distinguished guest, carried considerable prestige. Flourishing his sword, the carver slashed open the carcass, skewered the tastiest morsels and transferred them to the host's dish. Over time, the role became largely ceremonial. At Versailles, where he was known as Controller of the King's Pantry, the occupant of the office no longer touched the food. Accompanying dishes from the kitchen, he stood by with a sword while the royal family ate. Such positions changed hands for large sums, but the money was well spent. From what he observed while holding the post at Versailles under the free-spending Louis XV, playwright Pierre-Augustin Caron de Beaumarchais wrote *The Barber of Seville* and *The Marriage of Figaro*, classic views of the aristocracy as seen by their servants. Beaumarchais found Louis an inviting target for satire. "There was nothing he liked so much as flattery," wrote the Duc de Saint-Simon, "or, to put it more plainly, adulation. The coarser and clumsier it was, the more he relished it."

To feed the thousands of courtiers surrounding the king and his nobles, chefs augmented game with saltwater fish, oysters and lobsters, and pies and pastries made from the meat of hares, deer and wild birds. The "four and twenty blackbirds baked in a pie" of the nursery rhyme was no invention. Woodcocks, larks, thrushes, robins and cranes were all prized, as were pigeons. Servants stalked the roosting flocks at night, dazzling them with burning torches while they clubbed them to the ground, the subject of a striking 1874 painting, *Chasse des oiseaux avec les feux* (Hunting Birds With Fire), by Jean-François Millet.

Quail were also popular. A page from one of the most important Gothic manuscripts, created between 1412 and 1416 for John, Duke of Berry, shows the duke celebrating the New Year with heaped dishes of roasted quail, obviously meant to be eaten with the fingers. Successive generations of cooks developed new recipes for this delectable bird. By adding fruit, *caille aux raisins* (quail with grapes) tenderized its sometimes tough and dry flesh. For the more complex *cailles en sarcophage* (quails in a sarcophagus), the birds were boned

Bird's-Nesters, Jean-François Millet, 1874, Philadelphia Museum of Art

and baked in a shell of puff pastry with truffles and *foie gras*. Danish writer Karen Blixen resurrected this long-forgotten dish, a speciality of Paris's Café Anglais, for her 1950 short story *Babette's Feast*, made world-famous by Gabriel Axel's Academy Award-winning 1987 film adaptation starring Stéphane Audran.

The more rare the bird, the more exotic the recipe. Ortolans, no bigger than a thumb and too tiny to shoot, were trapped in a mist net, drowned in cognac, roasted in a closed casserole and eaten whole, including feathers, head and feet. As larks were noted for their song, chefs served their tongues separately, cooked, since their sound was "sweet," in honey. The remaining meat became pâté, a particular favorite of American food writer M.F.K. Fisher. Reminiscing about her days in post-World War II France, she wrote, "There was always that little rich decadent tin of lark pâté in the cupboard if I grew bored."

Royal dinners ended with *mignardises*: sweet cakes, nuts coated in candy or fruits preserved by boiling in sugar. One of the earliest depictions of confectionery is in the 15th-century French hangings known as *The Lady and the Unicorn*, each tapestry illustrating one of the five senses. To convey the sense of taste, the lady is shown selecting a sweet from a dish offered by her maid, while a monkey at her feet nibbles on one it has stolen.

Anything sweet was generally flavored with honey. Sugar, like salt, was valued as a preservative, and taxed accordingly. (The levy on salt alone brought in six percent of France's total revenue.) Difficulties in refining and transporting cane sugar from the West Indies inflated its price to a level comparable to such spices as nutmeg,

The Lady and the Unicorn "Taste," between 1484 and 1500, Musée de Cluny in Paris

ginger and cloves. It remained there until the means were discovered at the start of the 19th century to extract sugar from beets.

Ritual dominated eating at Versailles and other palaces. Meals arrived at the table in waves of a dozen or more dishes at a time. Called *service à la française* (French service), this system survived until the early 19th century, when, largely at the instigation of the great chef Marie-Antoine Carême, it was supplanted by Russian service (*service à la russe*), in which each diner received a portion of the dish individually and at the same moment, a reflection of the fact that the czars had enough serfs to serve even a hundred guests simultaneously.

The tables on which royalty dined were generally oval or round. Favored courtiers sat close to the king and queen, and shared their privileged access to the food, while those farthest from the royal presence had to grab what they could. Everyone but the king wore full court dress at table, including a hat, and no dish could be touched until the king served himself. Dishes of salt were placed conveniently close to the king and his favorites. The remaining diners, in a phrase that came to mean anyone deprived of preference by reason of class, were considered "below the salt."

The king's feasts culminated in lavish entertainments. During his 72-year reign, Louis XIV, known as "The Sun King" for the lavishness of his court, commissioned more than 300 works of art, many documenting his leisure activities, including the hunt. Three thousand courtiers lived in and around the Palace of Versailles, including the playwright Molière and composer Jean-Baptiste Lully. (In a rare case among musicians of a work-related fatality, Lully, who beat time with a heavy staff, brought it down on his foot. The wound became infected, and he died of blood poisoning.) His banquet and events manager, the *Officier de Bouche* (Master of the Mouth), was required not only to feed as many as a thousand guests but also stage the accompanying spectacles. Festivals could last for days. Fireworks were commonplace, but Versailles went one better. At sunset, its gardens erupted with fountains. Water spouted, gushed and bubbled, artfully lit to show off the ingenuity of the royal engineers and the landscaping of André Le Nôtre. Musicians played pieces composed specifically for the spectacle, and for *masques,*

Festivity given by Louis XIV, at Versailles in 1674. Performance of the opera *Alceste* by Lully and Quinault, Jean Le Pautre, 1676

in which performers, often including Louis himself, dressed in sumptuous costumes to dance and act out a mythological story.

CHAPTER 5

FISHING FOR COMPLIMENTS

*François Vatel's suicide over
the disgrace of the missing fish*

I n 1671, the Duc de Condé, Louis XIV's uncle,
and for that reason properly addressed as *Monsieur
le Prince* (Mr. Prince), completed a major restoration
of his chateau at Chantilly. To celebrate, he invited
the 33-year-old king to inspect the improvements. The
monarch often made such excursions, accompanied by
a retinue. As well as showing provincial nobility that he
kept an eye on their activities, it relieved the strain on
the royal kitchens, and also promised good hunting.

Still Life with Lobster and Fruit, Abraham van Beyeren, early 1650s, Metropolitan Museum of Art

A courtier visited Chantilly to finalize the arrangements.

"His majesty doesn't want a fuss," he explained. "Just some quiet days in the country with a few old and close friends."

But Condé knew the king. "I assume this means his highness will expect food and entertainment of a lavishness to rival the Rome of the Caesars."

"Precisely."

"And how many 'old and close friends' may we expect?"

"A mere handful. No more than five or six hundred." Not to mention the several hundred valets, maids and servants who would attend them.

Summoning his *Officier de Bouche*, François Vatel, Condé ordered him to plan three banquets on consecutive nights, plus the two-hour spectacles of music, dance, theatrical illusions and fireworks that went with them.

Vatel rallied his troops. Just as a general seldom picks up a weapon, the Master of the Mouth prepared no food. After deciding on the menu, he briefed his *chef de cuisine*, who, likewise, did no actual cooking. (Vatel has been credited with the invention of only one dish, the sweet vanilla-flavored *crème Chantilly*, but this existed long before his time.) Seated in the middle of the kitchen, the chef supervised a team of butchers, pastry cooks, *sauciers* and, in particular, roasters. Skilled technicians who knew to a few seconds how long a fowl or fish should cook, these men supervised the three-meter-long spits that rotated before the flames, turned by sweating "spit boys" who sat in an alcove next to the open hearth and operated a crank or, in larger houses, a treadmill.

Although barely protected from the heat, these "boys," who worked six-hour shifts beginning at 4 a.m., did so fully clothed, nudity being considered lewd. Nor could they take a toilet break, since nothing must interrupt the steady rotation of the spitted meats. Once they left the kitchen, comfort was still denied them. Like all but the most senior servants, they slept on the floor. In an additional health risk, they were exposed to the effects of the charcoal increasingly used in the best kitchens to reduce smoke and maximize heat. A number of chefs died of carbon monoxide poisoning, among them the great Carême, cook to Napoleon's closest adviser, Talleyrand, and to Britain's Prince of Wales.

Louis and his party arrived at Chantilly on Thursday and were shown around the estate. After picnicking in a field of daffodils (planted for the occasion), they mounted

Louis XIV and His Court Hunting at the Château of Meudon, Adam Frans Van der Meulen (1632–1690), Versailles, Musée du Château

up and went in search of game. The hunt continued after sunset, the king pursuing a stag by moonlight. After this, they returned to the chateau for turtle soup, fried trout and roast pheasant, followed by fireworks. For Vatel, however, the evening ended in despair. Louis brought more people than expected, and there were not enough pheasants to go round. A few guests had to make do with chicken. Then it rained, dampening the fireworks intended as the climax of the evening.

Worse was to come. As Catholics ate no meat on Fridays, every dish for the second banquet had to be fish or vegetables. Pike and trout swam in Chantilly's ponds, but saltwater fish, oysters, lobsters and other crustaceans had to come from the Atlantic coast, more than 200 kilometres away. Vatel had purchased the entire day's catch at the nearest port, Boulogne-sur-Mer. Packed in seaweed and loaded into four-horse carts, each hauling 3.5 tonnes, it left at dusk. Fresh horses waited every 20 kilometres along the route. Even then, the trip in pitch darkness over unpaved roads took all night.

Descending from his apartments at 4 a.m. on Friday, Vatel stepped over his exhausted staff asleep along the corridors. At sunrise, an apprentice carried two baskets of fish into the kitchens: the estate's own fresh-water catch.

Vatel, hysterical with fatigue, demanded, "Is that all?"

When the flustered boy told him nothing else had arrived, Vatel began to rave. His friend, the Duc de Gourville, tried to calm him. But Vatel was beyond reason. "I will not survive this disgrace," he told de Gourville. "My honor and reputation are lost."

Later that day, Madame de Sévigné rushed off a letter to her daughter, describing what followed:

> *Vatel, the great Vatel, seeing that this morning at eight o'clock the fish had not arrived, and not being able to bear the dishonour by which he thought he was about to be struck—in one word, he stabbed himself. They sent for Monsieur le Prince, who is in utter despair. Monsieur le Duc [de Gourville] burst into tears. You can imagine the disorder which such a terrible accident caused at this fête. And imagine that just as he was dying, the fish arrived!*

Vatel was buried quietly on the estate. The location of his grave isn't known, although he is memorialized among the legends of culinary history as a chef for whom food was, literally, a matter of life and death.

CHAPTER 6

TOOLS
OF THE TRADE

But first, Louis XVI grabbed the choicest morsels with his fingers

*B*ecket, Jean Anouilh's 1959 play about the relationship between King Henry II of England and 12th-century Archbishop of Canterbury Thomas à Becket, includes a significant culinary detail.

"Tonight," says Becket, "you can do me the honour of christening my forks."

"Forks?" says the king.

"Yes, from Florence. New little invention. It's for pronging meat and carrying it to the mouth. It saves you dirtying your fingers."

"But then you dirty the fork."

"Yes, but it's washable."

Les Très Riches Heures du Duc de Berry (The Very Rich Hours of the Duke of Berry), Herman, Paul and Jean de Limbourg, 1413-16, Musée Condé, Chantilly

"So are your fingers," says the king. "I don't see the point."

Unless you're looking for it, one easily overlooks the sparseness of dining tables in early paintings of banquets. In Leonardo da Vinci's *The Last Supper*, painted around 1495, neither knives nor forks appear. The hard unleavened bread of the time wasn't cut but broken, a term that survives to this day: We still speak of hospitality as "breaking bread." In Brueghel's *The Peasant Wedding* of 1567, the only utensils are simple wooden-handled knives of the sort every man would have carried in his belt. From medieval times, a knife in its leather sheath, embossed with his family crest, was the indispensable accessory of any gentleman, second in importance only to his sword. According to the Provençal poet Frédéric Mistral, it was the custom for farmworkers to begin eating only when the farmer or overseer drew his knife. Returning it to his belt signalled that the meal was over.

Forks, as Anouilh suggests, began as an affectation of the rich, and were condemned by the church as unmanly. Some people, with memories of the Black Death, associated them with apocalyptic paintings of devils using tridents to torment the sinful in hell. When forks did appear, it was in small numbers, and so rarely that travelers often carried their own. Even then, they were used only to lift a piece of meat from the communal dish and transfer it to one's plate. After that, one ate with fingers, wiping them on one's clothes. One of the earliest signs of gracious eating was the introduction of napkins. A typical inventory of a 17th-century French household listed only 18 forks but 600 linen *serviettes*. At the table of Louis XVI, eating with one's fingers remained a prerogative of the king. Long after it had become customary for food to be taken from the dish with a fork and conveyed to one's plate, the king would dive into a dish and tear off the choicest morsels.

Glasses were also uncommon. With glassware so expensive, hosts kept it out of the greasy fingers of his guests. If someone wished to drink, he gestured for a servant who arrived with a goblet filled with wine. After the guest had slaked his thirst, usually in a single swallow known as a quaff, he handed back the glass, which was rinsed out for the next user.

As food became more complex, so did the tools needed to eat it and the manner in which they were used. Such codes of behavior became known by the French word *etiquette*, meaning a label or tag. To someone ignorant of these rules, the dining table was a social minefield. As well as specific glasses for red wine, white wine, water, *apéritifs* and *digestifs*, the basic knife, fork and spoon, known collectively as a *couvert,* multiplied. Ranged on either side of your plate, which itself came in a number of sizes, depending on the course being served, were knives for both meat and fish, another for buttering bread, a fork specifically for salads and spoons for both soup and dessert, not to mention tea and other beverages.

Finger bowls filled with water and meant to clean sticky or greasy fingers were an additional hazard. Ignorant diners, assuming they held a beverage or some kind of soup, sometimes drank them. The poet Sylvia Plath wrote in her novel *The Bell Jar*, "The water had a few cherry blossoms in it, and I thought it must be some clear sort of Japanese after-dinner soup and ate every bit of it, including the crisp little blossoms." Rather than show up Plath's ignorance of etiquette, her hostess did the same thing.

Eating with the fingers never entirely died out. It only took one aristocrat to break the rules for a practice to become fashionable again. The sandwich, that classic finger food, is believed to have been invented around 1772 by John Montagu, 4th Earl of Sandwich, who had cold beef between slices of bread brought to his desk (or, in some versions, the gaming table) rather than pause for a meal.

Around the same time, Louis XVI developed a taste for the gelatinous meat of pig's feet. Boiled for two days until the bones softened, they were best eaten with the fingers. Watching the king munch his way through a brace of trotters, and concerned about a return to the free-for-all of medieval banquets, the arbiters of etiquette dictated that, aside from pig's feet, a special case, it was acceptable to eat with one's fingers only those creatures that originally flew. Chicken legs and wings were permissible but not portions of rabbit and, in particular, not legs of mutton. The use of fingers survives in France. One tears bread rather than slicing it, and, on less formal occasions, using a piece of bread to mop up a sauce is regarded as a compliment to the chef.

It's also still usual to eat cake with one's fingers. One of the more ritualized examples involves the *galette des rois* or kings cake. A disc of puff pastry, rich in butter and filled with almond paste, the *galette* is traditionally eaten on January 6, the 12th night after Christmas, the feast of the Epiphany. Each *galette* comes with a golden paper crown, and, like its cousins the British Christmas pudding and the Hogmanay black bun of Scotland, contains a prize; a silver coin in the British and Scottish creations, but in the *galette* a china figurine known as a *fève* or lima bean. The person who finds the *fève* drops it into the glass of a child or lover, the crown is placed on that person's head,

Epiphany (Le Gâteau des rois), Jean-Baptiste Greuze, 1774, Musée Fabre

and to the shout *"le roi boit"* or *"la reine boit,"* (the king or queen drinks), everyone toasts the person's health.

The *galette des rois* has inspired many artists, mostly celebrating families bonding over the ritual. In Jean-Baptiste Greuze's *Le Gâteau des rois* of 1774, a peasant couple and their six children gather around the dining table as a toddler, held by the maid, is offered a slice of the *galette.* Among the most poignant uses was that made by Jacques Demy in his 1964 film *Les Parapluies de Cherbourg* (The Umbrellas of Cherbourg). Catherine Deneuve, pregnant and about to contract a loveless marriage, weeps as the cardboard crown is placed on her head, a symbol of the meaningless relationship to which she is being condemned.

CHAPTER 7

STILL LIVES

Jean-Baptiste-Siméon Chardin influences Matisse, Cézanne and Picasso

B ecause art school students began by drawing inanimate objects—jugs and jars, apples and pears, plaster casts of hands and feet—most avoided the still life or *nature morte* in their professional lives, particularly since the market for such paintings was vanishingly small. The form dwindled even more following the invention of photography, to the relief of most painters, who were glad to escape, as one put it, "the tyranny of the anecdote."

The Ray, Jean-Baptiste-Siméon Chardin, 1725–26, Musée du Louvre

An artist might be commissioned to paint a house or some other treasure as a permanent souvenir. Occasionally someone wanted paintings of fruit or flowers to brighten a home during winter, while compositions showing pheasants, hares or a turkey next to silver *objets d'art* reminded guests of their host's prosperity, social standing and skill in hunting.

In 1827, a former general of Napoleon, Charles Yves César Cyr du Coëtlosquet, commissioned Eugène Delacroix to create a painting for the dining room of his chateau. *Nature morte au homard* (Still Life with Lobster) shows two cooked lobsters lying on a dish, next to a pheasant, a jay and a hare. Nearby are a hunting rifle and a bag for carrying game. Inspired by a recent visit to England, Delacroix shows the dish sitting in a typical British landscape, with huntsmen in the distance. The painting has a sly political element. Unsympathetic with the general's right-wing views, Delacroix chose lobsters and other *gibier* as emblems of political conservatism.

It was rare for an artist to specialize in the *nature morte*. One who did, Jean-Baptiste-Siméon Chardin (1699–1779), was even more exceptional in possessing a technique and sensibility that would have made him a master no matter what his subject. According to his friend, the philosopher and critic Denis Diderot, "To look at pictures by other artists, it seems that I need to borrow a different pair of eyes. To look at those of Chardin, I only have to keep the eyes that nature gave me and make good use of them."

Chardin admired such Dutch masters as Vermeer for the pleasure they took in simple domestic objects. He painted bowls, jugs and dishes, the last frequently heaped

Saying Grace, Jean-Baptiste-Siméon Chardin, Salon of 1740, Musée du Louvre

with fruit. Almost nothing sold until Charles-André van Loo, a member of the Royal Academy and resoundingly successful because of his huge history paintings, visited by Place Dauphine, a quiet park on the Île de la Cité where Chardin's work was on show. Once van Loo bought a painting, the art world took a new interest. Applying for membership of the Academy in 1728, Chardin submitted two canvases of uncompromising simplicity. *La Raie* (The Ray) showed a table of seafood invaded by a greedy kitten, while in *Le Buffet* (The Buffet), a dining table is dominated by a bowl heaped with fruit.

Despite the bucolic character of his work, the Academy accepted him, but only after rigorous vetting. Chardin grumbled, "You can be sure that most of the high positions in the country would be empty if one were admitted only after an examination as severe as the one we painters must pass." Endorsement by the rest of the artistic establishment took longer. Some—probably correctly—saw his placid domestic interiors as an implied sneer at their images of battles and incidents in the life of Napoleon.

Chardin did eventually widen his choice of subjects, piqued by the comment of a friend, Jacques-André-Joseph Aved. Aved complained about the small fees he was offered for portraits. Chardin replied that one should never turn down a commission, no matter how poorly paid.

"Easy for you to say," Aved replied. "A portrait is harder to paint than a saveloy sausage."

Taking this as a challenge, Chardin started painting portraits. To the further irritation of his colleagues, however, he ignored the rich, who might have commissioned studies of themselves and their families. Instead, he painted their servants as they washed clothes, peeled vegetables, fetched water and took care of the master's children, whom Chardin shows as lazy, idling their time away, blowing bubbles, spinning tops or building houses of cards. These images confirmed the suspicion that Chardin was at least partly a social satirist, and his canvases an assault on a society which pursued pleasure but placed no value on domestic labor. Although Louis XV owned the 1740 *Le Bénédicité* (Saying Grace), showing a maid instructing the two children under her care to pray before eating, the implied criticism of moral decline probably went over his head.

More than a century after his death, the Impressionists, who shared his dislike of "story" paintings, "discovered" Chardin. As a student, Henri Matisse spent weeks in the Louvre, meticulously copying his work in order to analyze his style, while Paul Cézanne's studies of the natural world clearly owed something to the earlier master. In addition, Pablo Picasso painted his own versions of *La Raie* and other Chardin canvases.

Chardin also did a number of self-portraits, about which novelist Marcel Proust wrote with enthusiasm:

> *Above his enormous pince-nez that have slipped down to the end of his nose, which they grip with their two brand-new glass discs ... Way above them, lifeless eyes, with high, worn-out pupils that seem to have seen a lot, laughed a lot, loved a lot, and to say with a boastful, tender tone 'Well yes, I am old!' Beneath the lifeless softness that age has lent them, the eyes are still aflame. But the eyelids, tired as an over-used clasp, are red around the rim.*

Self-portrait with Spectacles
(1771) and *The Buffet* (1728),
Jean-Baptiste-Siméon
Chardin, Musée du Louvre

Proust was right to single out Chardin's eyes, since the painter's sight was progressively affected by the lead in his pigments. Once he could no longer use oils, he turned to pastels, at which he proved no less expert. When a colleague asked if he missed the colors of oil painting, Chardin replied, "Who told you one paints with colors? One makes use of pigments, but one paints with one's emotions."

CHAPTER 8

THE DINNER AT VARENNES

Gourmand King Louis XVI becomes prisoner of innkeeper Monsieur Sauce

O n the afternoon of July 14, 1789, as his subjects stormed Paris's prison, the Bastille, igniting the French Revolution, Louis XVI, ensconced 25 kilometres away in the palace of Versailles and ignorant of the events that would lead to his downfall as well as that of his family and the entire leisured class of France, updated his diary, summarizing the day in a single word—*"Rien"* (Nothing).

Return from Varennes. Arrival of Louis Seize in Paris, June 25, 1791, Jean Duplessis-Bertaux, 1791

To be fair to Louis, "Nothing" didn't mean the day was without incident, but rather that he had not hunted, and therefore killed no animal. In a culture that took pride in doing no work and pursuing only pleasure, hunting was one of the few activities in which the nobility could honorably indulge.

Long after the whole of France was swept by intimations of revolt, Louis believed it was just a short-lived protest by radicals about the high price of bread. In July 1788, hailstorms had destroyed almost the entire harvest. In the winter that followed, canals and rivers froze, paralyzing the traffic in grain and cutting off supplies to the mills that ground it to flour. Grain stored for too long in damp conditions often spoiled. Any flour made from this wheat appeared yellow, smelled bad and could carry the poisonous fungus ergot that caused Saint Anthony's Fire, a severe burning sensation in the limbs. Most of it was used to make alcohol.

In the summer of 1787, a two-kilo loaf of bread cost eight sous. Following the failed harvest of 1788, the price rose to 12, and by February 1789 reached 15. At a time when a family of four needed two loaves a day to survive, the average working man was paid only about 30 sous a day. To stretch their supplies, bakers adulterated wheat flour with other grains, such as millet, and even added sawdust. Barefoot, mobs of Parisians walked to Versailles and gathered at the gates, demanding the king release grain from the royal granaries.

According to legend, Marie Antoinette asked a servant why they were shouting.

"They have no bread, your highness."

All this fuss because they had no toast for breakfast? "In that case," the queen is supposed to have said, "why not eat brioche?" (Somewhere between cake and bread, brioche was part of the royal *petit déjeuner.*) An Italian princess actually made this remark two generations before. Nor was it the sort of thing Marie Antoinette would have said. Being Austrian, she had a more cosmopolitan view of European cuisine than most French people.

Marie Antoinette was indirectly responsible for introducing the potato into France. Known since Columbus brought it back from the New World three centuries before, it was shunned as inedible because of its association with the earth until its champion, Antoine-Augustin Parmentier, persuaded the king and queen to take an interest. Marie Antoinette planted some at Versailles, and wore their white flowers in her hair. Encouraged by this patronage, Parmentier hosted a dinner that used potatoes in 20 different dishes. He also planted fields of potatoes in the Bois de Boulogne, ostentatiously placing guards so that people, thinking the plants and tubers valuable, would steal them. When the wheat harvest failed in 1787, the peasants ironically had potatoes

Antoine-Augustin Parmentier presenting a potato plant to Louis XVI and Marie Antoinette, *Le Petit Journal,,* 1901

on which to fall back, and thus survived to depose Louis and Marie Antoinette two years later.

Seeing no quick solution to the nation's problems, Louis's advisers urged him to flee. After dragging his feet until June 1791, Louis set out for Belgium, where he'd been told a force of loyal troops waited at the town of Montmédy, ready to lead a counterrevolution. The attempted escape was monumentally inept. Disguised unconvincingly as conventional ladies and gentlemen, the royal family and a retinue of courtiers set out in a caravan of carriages. Even then, they might have succeeded had Louis not insisted on using the most lavish of the regal coaches, so heavy that, on the first day, they only got as far as Varennes, 200 kilometers from Paris.

There, an alert innkeeper recognized the king, who was placed under house arrest by the local prosecutor, Jean-Baptiste Sauce. When he didn't return immediately to Paris, stories circulated that the famously greedy monarch was not so much Sauce's prisoner as his guest. According to gossip, the king took a liking to the local cheese, and even toasted M. Sauce with his own burgundy. Each new report, true or false, further eroded the respect in which Louis was held. On the gates of the Tuileries Palace, his Paris residence, someone who knew his tastes in meat hung a sign announcing "Lost Pig" and offering a reward for its return.

The king under arrest, and by the hand of a man named, of all things, Sauce, was a gift to the *feuilletonistes,* whose insulting reports and satirical cartoons were peddled by the *bouquinistes* along the Seine. One anonymous lithograph, *The Glutton, or Big Birds Fly Slowly,* showed the royal family resting at Varennes.

The Glutton, or Big Birds Fly Slowly, anonymous lithograph

Ignoring framed pictures on the wall of the fall of the Bastille that show he's in a revolutionary stronghold, Louis tears into a chicken with his bare hands. Prosecutor Sauce, drawn with the narrow face and pointed nose of the leading revolutionary, Maximilien de Robespierre, tries to serve an arrest warrant. "I don't give a fuck about all that," says Louis. "Let me eat in peace." Across the room, Marie Antoinette, admiring herself in the mirror—she was notoriously vain—says, "My dear Louis, you've already eaten two turkeys and drunk ten bottles of wine, when you know we are going to have dinner at Montmédy."

Taken back to Paris under guard, the royal family was imprisoned in the Tuileries Palace. Their flight changed public attitudes to the king, who, in trying to escape, showed he would never accept the changes demanded by the revolution. Within two years, he and his wife, along with thousands of men, women and children, would die on the guillotine.

CHAPTER 9

A PAINTER IN A PEAR TREE

*Cézanne conquers Paris
with an apple*

D etermined to make all new, the revolutionaries
of 1789 reorganized the calendar, dividing
the year into 13 parts. Discarding the former
names of the months, all of which derived from imperial
Rome, the poet, actor and playwright Fabre d'Églantine,
assisted by André Thouin from Paris's Jardin des Plantes,
invented new titles that reflected the character of
the season. The time when seeds germinated became
Germinal and the season of flowers Floréal. July was

Still Life with Apples and Pears, Paul Cézanne, c.1891–92, The Metropolitan Museum of Art

Thermidor, the month of heat, while August re-emerged as Fructidor, the time of fruit.

When Napoleon came to power, he rescinded the new calendar. It survives only in such fragments as Lobster Thermidor, a dish invented by the great chef Escoffier in which English mustard adds an incendiary edge to wine sauce. Émile Zola's 1885 novel *Germinal* compares a strike among coal miners to the sprouting of a new crop. "Men were springing forth, a black avenging army, germinating slowly in the furrows, growing towards the harvests of the next century, and their germination would soon overturn the earth."

The name Fructidor acknowledged the references to fruit that permeate French language and art. "To have the peach" *(avoir la pêche)* is to be in high spirits, "to show a banana" *(avoir la banane)* indicates a big smile, to "bring your strawberry" *(ramener sa fraise)* means to interrupt a conversation, equivalent to "putting in your two cents' worth," while to be compared to "the height of three apples" *(haut comme trois pommes)* means you are exceptionally short. As for "a stroll among the strawberries" *(aller aux fraises),* this is shorthand for one of those erotic afternoon interludes also known as *siestes crapuleuses.*

For artists, too, fruit can have a significance far beyond that of simple food. Paul Cézanne, believing that every product of nature displayed some aspect of the divine, would contemplate a landscape or still life for hours until its mystical topology became clear. Seen with this degree of intensity, even a piece of fruit could display cosmic significance. Arriving in the capital from his

Peeling a pear. cartoon in *Le Rire*, 1933

native Aix-en-Provence, Cézanne had startled everyone by announcing, "I will conquer Paris with an apple!"

Other artists found inspiration in the downy surface of a peach and the drooping richness of grapes. None, however, proved as seductive as the gravid bulk and autumnal tint of the pear. Erik Satie's *Trois morceaux*

en forme de poire (Three Pieces in the Form of a Pear),
a suite for two pianos, is divided, with an eccentricity
typical of Satie, not into three pieces but seven. If
business is discussed over a meal, it must be toward
the conclusion, *entre la poire et le fromage* (between the
pear and the cheese). "Are you paying my pear? *(Tu
te payes ma poire?)* means "Are you pulling my leg?"
Couper la poire en deux (to cut the pear in two) means to
compromise.

To call someone *un poire* is to label them a
dope. An apparently innocent cartoon in a 1933 issue
of the magazine *Le Rire* (The Laugh) shows a woman
peeling a pear, employing the elegant style affected in
high society, impaling it on a fork and rotating it while
removing the skin with a fruit knife. Her companions
are admiring.

"You have good manners," comments one.

"My boyfriend is a banker," she replies.

"Ah," says the friend. "It must have been he who
taught you how to skin pears so well."

In the depths of the Great Depression, this crack
about the greedy financial sector and its fleecing of the
innocent would have been instantly understood.

Cézanne, Picasso and numerous other artists
painted pears and pear trees. During an 1883 visit to
Arles, they inspired Vincent van Gogh—in particular, a
small and crooked *poirier,* his painting of which became
the centerpiece of an orchard triptych for the apartment
of his brother Theo. The annual miracle of flowering fruit
trees reminded him, he said, that a "man who finally
produces something poignant as the blossom of a hard,
difficult life, is a wonder, like the black hawthorn, or

Small Pear Tree in Blossom, Vincent van Gogh, 1888,
Van Gogh Museum, Amsterdam

better still the gnarled old apple tree which at certain
moments bears blossoms which are among the most
delicate and virginal things under the sun."

Seasonality is the key concept in the French
artist's attitude to fruit. Apples, characteristic of northern
Europe, and particularly England, will, correctly stored,
keep for months, unlike those fruits of the warm south—

peaches, cherries, figs and melons—which survive only a few days of summer heat. When 19th-century Parisians wanted fruit, they often picked it for themselves. Certain villages on the outskirts of Paris were noted for their orchards: Argenteuil for figs, Montmorency for cherries, Vaugirard for strawberries. In season, city people rented a tree for the day and, sitting under it, stuffed themselves. After the harvest, teams of gleaners moved in, plucking the high-hanging fruit left by the professionals as too difficult to reach.

Until refrigeration, getting fruit to the public remained a perennial problem, wittily addressed by the Belgian author Simon Leys in his 1986 novella *La Mort de Napoléon* (The Death of Napoleon). Leys imagines the emperor escaping from Saint Helena, leaving a lookalike to be buried in his place. Incognito in Paris, he's sheltered by a woman who owns a string of fruit barrows. When a glut of ripe melons offers her a large profit if she can sell them within a day, Napoleon employs his military skills, brilliantly rallying a team of helpers to distribute them.

Tropical fruit was rare in Europe until long after World War II. The postwar reappearance of bananas marked the end of austerity, but other fruit awaited large-scale refrigeration. Until then, in such works as *Le Rêve transformé* (The Dream Transformed) and the painting of Montparnasse railway depot he called *Gare Montparnasse: The Melancholy of Departure* (1913 and 1914 respectively), Italian Surrealist Giorgio de Chirico used bunches of bananas, green or ripe, to signify desire, satisfied or thwarted.

The first pineapples arrived with émigrés from France's African colonies, Morocco, Algeria and Senegal, but their oranges and dates seldom reached France except at Christmas. Dates, dried and preserved, still on their stalks, are a traditional holiday delicacy in France, along with tangerines from Sicily. In both cases, appearance counts for more than taste. Sweeter and juicier citrus exists than the Sicilian variety, but the hard, often bitter fruit, each with a stem and a few dark green leaves attached, are preferred, the pungency of their skins a seasonal reminder, like the dates, of biblical oases where the Three Kings of Orient might have rested in their search for the Messiah.

A poignant use of fruit in art comes in *Le Temps des cerises* (The Time of Cherries), a song of 1866 associated with the brief anarchist rising known as the Commune. In the political vacuum following the Franco-Prussian War, the people of Montmartre, the most belligerent and socialist of Paris's districts, realized that the city was theirs for the taking. Fortifying their hilltop village, they declared Paris a free city, and set about correcting the abuses of Emperor Napoleon III's corrupt rule. Workers were encouraged to take over factories abandoned by their owners, and a moratorium on debt allowed artisans to retrieve tools pawned to feed their families. War widows were voted a pension, children out of wedlock accorded the same rights as those born in marriage, the church ejected from education, and secular schools set up to teach a more liberal curriculum.

For a while, it seemed the communards would get away with it. Troops sent in to subdue them refused

Women picking figs, Cover of *Nouveaux Pauvres* (The New Poor). Illustration by Maurice Colineau, 1929

to fire on their own neighbors and instead shot their generals. Men and women danced and sang in the streets, their anthem *Le Temps des cerises:*

> *When we sing the time of cherries,*
> *Gay nightingale and mocking blackbird*
> *Will both celebrate.*
> *The beautiful will go crazy*
> *And lovers have sun in their hearts*

The dreams of the Commune, like those of the revolution, withered in the chill of political reality. New troops recruited in the south, without allegiances to the Montmartrois, were brought in. Smuggled behind the lines through mine workings, they crushed the amateur rebellion. In the *Semaine Sanglante* or Bloody Week that followed, hundreds of thousands of men and women were executed or deported to New Caledonia. The red of cherries was compared to the blood they shed. *Le Temps de cerises* acquired a despairing final verse:

> *I shall always love the time of cherries.*
> *It's a time I keep in my heart,*
> *An open wound.*

CHAPTER 10

THE HUMBLER POISONS

"Come quickly, I am tasting the stars!"—Dom Pérignon

Though it had been known since the Stone Age that sugary liquids, left for long periods in the dark, fermented and became alcoholic, winemaking only arrived in France in the first century AD, brought by the Romans. When their empire contracted, there was a real risk that this skill, like many others, would perish. Fortunately, the church took up the task. Ostensibly it did so in order to guarantee supplies of wine to be drunk during the mass, but religious uses

An abbey cellarer testing his wine. Illumination from a copy of *Li livres dou santé* by Aldobrandino of Siena. late 13th century

counted for only a tiny fraction of production. Most was sold to the nobility, to whom the appeal was obvious. The alcoholic level of beer, the drink of the common people, peaked at four percent, and only half that for "small" beer, made from grain being used for the second time, while wine boasted a robust 16 percent.

Most countries identified wine by the variety of grape from which it was made—Chardonnay, Merlot, Pinot Noir, Cabernet Sauvignon—but France's intimate relationship with the *terroir* or soil led to wines being named for the district that produced them. In Burgundy, Cistercian and Benedictine abbeys perfected a light red wine that was exported under that name throughout Europe. British litterateur and wit Samuel Johnson dismissed this "claret," as the English called it, as "poor stuff: the liquor for boys." Men, he believed, should stick to port, "but he who aspires to be a hero must drink brandy."

Brandy, too, was a French invention. Monks in Charente, the district on the Atlantic coast above Bordeaux, discovered distillation early in the 16th century. Experimenting with ways to reduce the volume of wine, both to simplify shipping and minimize taxes, they heated it in a copper vessel known as an alembic. Since alcohol evaporated at a lower temperature than water, the process created a concentrate they called *brandewijn*—"burnt wine" in Dutch—soon shortened to "brandy." Other vignerons reused leftover seeds, stems and skins to produce an even more powerful and rougher spirit called *marc*.

These new and potent spirits, known as *eaux de vie* (waters of life), contained as much as 60 percent alcohol.

Following the practice of winemakers, distillers named their products for the district where they were created. The Charentais towns of Cognac and Armagnac provided names for the main varieties of grape brandy, while the apple-scented spirit distilled from cider acquired the name of the Norman *département* of Calvados.

Such serious drinkers as Samuel Johnson liked their brandy neat, but some Charentais producers, with the social drinker in mind, mixed cognac with fermented grape juice to make Pineau des Charentes, while Calvados blended with apple juice became Pommeau. Elsewhere, monks infused the pure spirit with flowers and herbs to create "fortified" wines or cordials. These were drunk before meals, supposedly to stimulate appetite—*apéritifs*—or, after eating, as *digestifs*, to aid digestion. Among the most famous was Chartreuse, developed at the monastery of that name near Grenoble. One hundred and thirty herbs and flowers gave the liqueur a distinctive yellow-green tint that became a color in its own right. By the early 20th century, these cordials numbered in the hundreds. In Scott Fitzgerald's *Tender Is the Night*, Dick Diver contemplates the contents of a cocktail bar: "the humbler poisons of France— bottles of Otard, Rhum St. James, Marie Brizard, Punch Orangeade, André Fernet Branca, Cherry Rocher, and Armagnac."

The practice of naming a wine for its district rather than the grape that produced it developed into the system known as *Appellation d'Origine Contrôlée,* which required vignerons to identify where their grapes were grown, and limited the amount of wine sold. The AOC protected the reputation and good name of wines

The famous cellerier Dom Pérignon (1638-1715) tasting the grapes of the vineyards of the Abbey of Hautvillers, property of the house of Moët & Chandon since 1794, José Frappa

that might otherwise be undermined by indiscriminate production for profit.

Wines produced in the valleys of the Rhône and Gironde in the southeast were christened Bordeaux, after the largest city of the region, while a dry white wine, naturally effervescent, associated with the cooler climate of the northeast, took the name of that district, Champagne.

A Benedictine monk, Dom Pierre Pérignon (1638–1715), cellar-master at the abbey of Hautvilliers, near Épernay, is often credited with inventing champagne. According to legend, his first sip of the sparkling wine so delighted him that he called to his fellow monks, "Come

quickly, I am tasting the stars!" In fact, champagne was
known to the Romans, though Pérignon did pioneer
many techniques still used in its creation, including
the *méthode champenoise*. In this system, bottles of
young wine, stored in sloping racks, cork down, are
turned periodically by hand. From time to time, the
cork is removed, a little wine drawn off, along with any
sediment, sugar added to increase clarity and sparkle, and
the bottle recorked.

That some winemakers, including members of the
clergy, would indulge to excess in sampling their product
was accepted as a *risque du métier*. Early European
drinking songs gave a featured role to the alcoholism of
monks, priests, even the pope. One such poem, the 13th-
century *In Taberna Quando Sumus* (When We Are in the
Tavern), was used by Carl Orff in his oratorio *Carmina
Burana:*

> *To the Pope and to the King,*
> *Unrestrained the tankards ring.*
> *Drinks the young 'un, and the old 'un,*
> *Drinks the bishop and the deacon,*

Today, vintage Dom Pérignon sells at prices that
would have astonished the modest monk. In 2008, three
magnums dating from 1966, 1973 and 1976, fetched
$93,260 and two bottles of the legendary Rosé Vintage
1959 sold for $84,700.

After four centuries, champagne remains an
indispensable accompaniment to any important social
occasion. In launching a new enterprise, from a ship
to a shop, the occasion is incomplete until a bottle of
champagne is shattered, a contemporary equivalent of

The champagne cave of Épernay, André Galland, 1937

a sacrifice to the gods. Celebrations of the wine itself
range from the decision of composers Alan Jay Lerner
and Frederick Loewe, in adapting Colette's novel
Gigi into a musical, to write *The Night They Invented
Champagne*, and, between the wars, French artist André

Galland to paint the cathedral-like caverns at Épernay in a way that evoked a mysterious, even slightly sinister world, at odds with the attraction of the product.

In *belle époque* Paris, the city's most select bordello, Le Chabanais, kept a richly decorated metal bath for the exclusive use of the Prince of Wales, son of Queen Victoria and future King Edward VII, and a regular client of this *maison close*. For his highness, the bath was filled with champagne and one of the establishment's most beautiful women directed to bathe in it while the heir to the British throne and his cronies sat around, filling their glasses from the uniquely flavored wine.

At the same time, across the city, at Maxim's, Lapérouse or any of the other restaurants where the wealthy pleasure-seekers gathered, men toasted their companions of the night in champagne drunk from their satin-lined slippers. This somewhat unsanitary tradition reappeared in automobile racing. Squirting fellow drivers and members of the crowd with champagne from a briskly shaken jeroboam has long been a tradition of Formula One prize-giving ceremonies, but Australian driver Daniel Ricciardo went one better, pioneering what he calls a "shoey," honoring his fellow drivers by drinking champagne from his sweaty footwear.

CHAPTER 11

CHEESE AS A NATIONAL SYMBOL

"How can you govern a country that has 246 varieties of cheese?"
—Charles de Gaulle

For centuries, cheese in its many hundreds of forms, eaten with a crusty baguette and a glass of red wine, has been the midday meal for a sizable percentage of France. Not only did this combination of protein and carbohydrate provide energy for a day

Cheese pavilion at Les Halles in Paris, c.1900

of hard labor; the choice of a cheese from your home district could affirm one's cultural identity.

From the Middle Ages, cheese was a primary source of protein for the peasantry. Typically, it contains about 30 percent protein and 30 percent fat, almost the same as red meat, and substantially more than vegetables with their mere one percent to five percent protein. Cheese had the added advantage of simplicity. It could be manufactured in the poorest kitchen with the simplest ingredients. Rennet, found in the stomach of a cow, and in certain plants, such as the thistle or fig, was added to milk, which separated into solids—curds—and a watery residue—whey. Pressed into a mold and left to cure, the curds turned to cheese, soft or hard depending on how long they were left to mature.

Variants soon appeared. The use of cow, goat or sheep milk created the subgroups of *vache, chèvre* and *brebis.* To preserve cheeses and add flavor, they were wrapped in vine leaves, rolled in herbs, peppercorns, dried fruits or ashes, or flavored with such seeds as caraway, cumin or anise. Novelist Honoré de Balzac described approvingly "the famous cheese of the Touraine and du Berry, made with goats' milk and reproducing on its surface the pattern of the vine leaves in which it had been molded, and which replicated the style of Touraine engravings."

Blue cheese developed when naturally occurring bacteria, usually by chance, found their way into soft cheese. Roquefort, the most famous blue, was supposedly discovered by accident in the caves of Roquefort-sur-Soulzon, in the rocky southern region of Aveyron. According to legend, a farm boy, distracted by a village maiden, left his lunch in the cave. Chancing on the leftovers some weeks later, he was surprised to find the cheese marbled with a blue mold that imparted a distinctive flavor. Although the mold has since been synthesized, the best Roquefort still matures in caverns where the culture occurs naturally.

The rise of cheese from one element in the French diet to a national symbol began early in the 19th century. In a nation with roughly the same population as the British Isles but many times the area, rural values predominated. With sugar expensive, hosts preferred to end a meal with cheese. Jean Anthelme Brillat-Savarin had already decreed, memorably, that "a meal without wine is like a day without sunshine." Now he added that "a dessert without cheese is like a beauty with only one eye."

The gastronomes of Britain and Holland, where cheeses were generally hard and neutral in aroma, deprecated the pungency and deliquescence of the predominantly soft and odiferous French product. James Joyce, an enthusiast for most foods, excluded cheese. "A corpse is meat gone bad," he sneered. "Well, and what's cheese? Corpse of milk." French authors were more appreciative. In his 1873 novel *Le Ventre de Paris* (The Belly of Paris), set around the teeming food market of Les Halles, Émile Zola rejoiced in cheese's variety:

> *The heat of the afternoon had softened the cheeses.*
> *The patches of mold on their crusts were melting, and*
> *glistening with tints of ruddy bronze and verdigris.*
> *Beneath their cover of leaves, the skins of the Olivets*
> *seemed to be heaving as with the slow deep respiration*

of a sleeping man. A Livarot was swarming with
life, and in a fragile box behind the scales a Gérome
flavored with aniseed diffused such a pestilential smell
that all around the very flies had fallen lifeless on the
grey-veined slab of ruddy marble.

This proliferation of regional cheeses created a connoisseurship rivaling that of wine. In 1925, the dairy industry adopted the wine industry's *Appellation d'Origine Contrôlée*, with Roquefort the first recipient. (Today, it specifically protects the names of 56 cheeses.)

As Paris became increasingly cosmopolitan, cheese entered the urban diet. Inner city producers kept livestock in their courtyards and roamed the streets to sell their product. As late as 1927, Janet Flanner, correspondent for *The New Yorker* magazine, wrote of "goatherds, including our favorite Baptiste, whose flock parades the Quartier St. Germain at high noon." She relished, in particular, his homemade *chèvre,* "at two [francs] fifty the cake, a remarkable luncheon dainty."

The variety of French cheeses and the fact that many existed only where geography, climate and raw materials occurred in unique combination made them a useful symbol of unity in diversity. A *fromager* could even acquire political influence. As, traditionally, the Paris cheese shop of Nicole Barthélémy supplied the presidential palace, journalists learned to watch the shop for signs of changes in the seats of power. If the government looked like resigning, a flunkey was sent to settle Barthelémy's bill, for fear the owner might cut off their credit.

Goat's milk and cheese seller with customer in January 1929 in Paris

In 1962, as the Communists launched a bid
for power, Charles de Gaulle derided their vision of a
one-party France, demanding, *"Comment voulez-vous
gouverner un pays qui a deux cent quarante-six variétés
de fromage?"* ("How can you govern a country that has
246 varieties of cheese?") His political judgment was
acute—the Communists never looked like winning—but
not his count of cheeses, estimated by some as more than
a thousand, and still rising.

CHAPTER 12

THE RISE OF THE RESTAURANT

Still open: Le Grand Véfour, which served Victor Hugo, Napoleon, Josephine, George Sand, Colette and Jean Cocteau

The golden age of restaurants began with the Revolution of 1789, when *chefs de cuisine* who had served the great houses of France found themselves out of work, and set up in business for themselves. Before then, travelers ate at inns that offered a plate of whatever the owner's wife had prepared that day; usually pottage, with bread and beer, which was eaten at a common table. Others brought food from

Le Déjeuner des canotiers (Luncheon of the Boating Party), Pierre-Auguste Renoir, 1880–81, The Phillips Collection

home or, when passing through a town, purchased bread, smoked meat, cheese and beer from a *boulanger, charcutier, fromager* and *brasseur,* eating them at the roadside.

Despite rival claims on behalf of Roze de Chantoiseau, who was running an establishment near the rue St. Honoré in 1773, France's first restaurateur is long believed to have been a M. Boulanger, who opened for business in 1765 on the corner of rue Bailleul and rue Pouille (today's rue du Louvre). He offered mostly *bouillons,* designed to *restaurer* or restore the weary traveler. An inscription by the door promised, *"Boulanger débite des restaurants divins"* (Boulanger provides divine restoratives). Some reports mention an additional quotation in Latin paraphrased from the Bible: *"Venite ad me omnes qui stomacho laboratis et ego vos restauro."* (Come to me those who are famished, and I will restore you.)

The luxury of choosing from a number of dishes, or sitting indoors at separate tables rather on a common bench, and enjoying the attention of competent waiters, including, apparently, Boulanger's pretty wife, was new to French culture. Encouraged, Boulanger was said to have introduced dishes other than soup, including "salted poultry and fresh eggs," and lamb's feet in white sauce, a precursor of *pieds d'agneau sauce poulette*, a sophisticated dish by any standards. Some accounts even have Boulanger standing in front of his establishment, dressed like a gentleman, complete with sword, and encouraging pedestrians to step inside.

Despite this accumulation of detail, recent research has cast doubt on the very existence of M. Boulanger. No

*The Corner of the Rue Bailleul and the Rue Jean Tison,
1831*, Thomas Shotter Boys, Musée Carnavalet

contemporary source mentions him or his establishment.
But whether he existed or not, the institution he
represented had come to stay. Dismissing protests from
shopkeepers of the food guilds who regarded them
as unfair competition, in June 1786 the Provost of
Paris issued a decree according restaurants legal status,
authorizing them to offer meals until 11 in the evening
in winter and midnight in summer.

The same year, Antoine Beauvilliers, former chef
to the Count de Provence, opened the Grande Taverne
de Londres. At mahogany tables with linen tablecloths,
under crystal chandeliers, efficient waiters served diners
from an extensive menu and wine list. Since, then as
now, "location, location, location" were the first rules
of any business, Beauvilliers shrewdly chose to open at
the Palais-Royal. Situated just opposite the Louvre, the
Palais was famous, indeed notorious, for its large formal

gardens and a surrounding arcade that sheltered shops, gambling rooms and a floating population of petty criminals, political plotters and prostitutes.

Today, the only surviving restaurant of any age at the Palais-Royal is Le Grand Véfour. Opened in 1784 as the Café de Chartres, it was purchased in 1820 by Jean Véfour, who gave it his name. Brass plates set into the tabletops record some of the celebrities who ate there, ranging from novelist Victor Hugo and gastronome Jean Anthelme Brillat-Savarin to Napoleon Bonaparte and his empress, Josephine. Cross-dressing novelist George Sand was such a regular customer that the restaurant made a cast of her hand to create its ashtrays. The aging Colette, who lived nearby, was regularly carried down the stairs to dine there, often with her neighbor Jean Cocteau, who designed its menus.

The working class of urban Paris seldom patronized restaurants, preferring street vendors who sold coffee, hot milk, bread, soup, roast potatoes and stew. Around noon on weekdays, pop-up restaurants appeared. Firing up stoves in otherwise empty stores, women prepared a few basic dishes which one could eat there or take away. Writing in 1899, Georges Montorgueil described one such woman:

> *There she kept her eye on her pot au feu* (beef and vegetables in broth) *while peeling the potatoes that sizzled in boiling fat—the same fat that served to deep-fry a sole, or cheese puffs and donuts. A sign proposed "Soup and Beef To Go." For two sous, you got a bowl of hot beef broth; for four more, you could*

Le No. 113, Palais-Royal, Georg Emanuel Opitz

choose between stewed beef, mussels, boiled potatoes—
and always, naturally, the classic frites.

For those who preferred cold cuts, *triperies*
offered cooked tongue and tripe. *Charcuteries* sold ham
and sausage, all of which could be eaten on the run, as
could bread still warm from the oven. Young men and
women still nibble the end of a baguette as they check
their smartphones while walking back to the office, and
a *sandwich jambon fromage*—ham and Gruyère cheese
on a baguette—remains the most popular lunchtime
snack.

Artists of the 16th century such as Titian and
Giorgione celebrated the French landscape by showing
gods and goddesses, nymphs and shepherds enjoying the
pleasures of the countryside, usually in the form of the
fête champêtre, an elaborate court picnic, with courtiers
in fancy dress, an orchestra hidden in the trees and
a lavish buffet lunch. When the Impressionists at the
end of the 19th century took art out of the studio and
began painting *en plein air,* they revisited such paintings,
but with a sarcastic edge. For his 1863 *Déjeuner sur
l'herbe* (Lunch on the Grass), Édouard Manet copied a
composition from Raphael. Two men and two women
recline in a forest setting, the men fully clothed, with
one woman nude and the other, half-dressed, wading
in a pond. Setting out to jar his audience by mixing
classical form and modern sensibility, Manet distorted the
proportions and perspective, giving the impression of an
outdoor scene recreated indoors. The remains of a picnic
add the last incongruous touch. The gods of Poussin and

Déjeuner sur l'herbe (Lunch on the Grass), Édouard Manet, 1862-63, Musée d'Orsay

Giorgione would never have lowered themselves to snack on bread and cheese.

Pierre-Auguste Renoir shared the common enjoyment of picnics, but painted them to emphasize their social rather than culinary pleasures. For his 1875 *Déjeuner chez Fournaise* (Lunch at Restaurant Fournaise), and the famous 1881 *Le Déjeuner des canotiers* (Luncheon of the Boating Party), he reproduced scenes at the Restaurant Fournaise at Chatou, a short boat ride along the Seine. In 1936, Jean Renoir, the painter's filmmaker son, directed *Une partie de campagne* (A Day in the Country), a 40-minute adaptation of a story by Guy de Maupassant about a naive shopkeeper and his son-in-law who succumb to the pleasures of an afternoon by the river, the men sleeping off their lunch while the wife and daughter surrender to the sensual attentions of two young city gents. As in Manet's canvas, the apparent innocence of a picnic is subborned by hints of classical abandon, one young man imitating a capering pipe-playing Pan as he lures the complaisant matron into the undergrowth.

In 1959, Jean Renoir enlarged on this theme in his fantasy of the near future, also called *Le Déjeuner sur l'herbe* (Lunch on the Grass). To publicize his views that artificial insemination should replace sex, a radical biologist stages a country picnic to announce his plans. Filmed around Cagnes-sur-Mer and at Les Collettes, the estate where Pierre-Auguste Renoir spent his last years, the film celebrates all the animal pleasures, not least those of eating and drinking *en plein air*. In adding a goat-herding Pan figure who can impose chaos with a few notes on his pipes, Renoir follows his father in sweeping away the social conventions associated with life lived in the open. "Invaded," in Renoir's words, "by far from scientific emotions," the biologist discards his convictions when he sees a beautiful peasant girl bathing in the nude and is seized with the desire to impregnate her.

CHAPTER 13

THE BLOOD OF LIFE

"I live on good soup, not on fine words."—Molière

King Henry IV is famous for having promised his subjects at least one good meal a week. *"Si Dieu me prête vie,"* he said, *"je ferai qu'il n'y aura point de laboureur en mon royaume qui n'ait les moyens d'avoir le dimanche une poule dans son pot!"* ("If God gives me life, I will make sure that no peasant in my realm will lack the means to have a fowl in his pot on Sunday!") Specifying *poule* and *pot* was significant. Listeners would have understood that, in speaking of a bird cooked in a

Bouillon restaurant, c.1860s

pot rather than on a spit, and a *poule* or hen rather than a *poulet* or chicken, Henry wasn't referring to a tender roasted bird but rather to an old fowl which, after a life of laying, became the basis of soup.

Lacking the ovens and spits found only in great houses, peasants cooked at the hearth, usually in an iron pot suspended over coals. During hours of simmering, even the toughest bird dissolved into the rich stock known as *bouillon,* without which no soup deserved the name. Adding cabbage, dried beans, turnips, carrots, potatoes and a handful or two of barley, the country wife made a soup substantial enough to feed an entire family. Rather than waste a drop, many followed the custom of *chabrot,* pouring a glass of red wine into the dregs to swill out the last morsels, a habit in part blamed for France's ubiquitous alcoholism.

At a time when bread was known as "the staff of life," *bouillon,* both food and medicine, was regarded as its blood. "I live on good soup, not on fine words," said the playwright Molière. Scottish writer Tobias Smollett, traveling in Provence in the 1760s, was offered *bouillon* as a treatment for tuberculosis. Locals swore it contained enough food value to revive even a man who'd been hanged.

The quality of *bouillon* lay in bones. Discarded by butchers, these were collected by provident cooks who baked them to drive the fat from the marrow, aromatized them with onions and garlic, then simmered them for hours to create a rich and nutritious stock. To skimp on this foundation, diluting or adulterating it, was an offense not only against taste and hospitality but also health. Honoré de Balzac in his 1842 novel *La Rabouilleuse* (The

Cooking in a pot from *Le Christ chez Marthe et Marie* (detail), Jos Goemaer, c.1600

Black Sheep) sneers at a cheap host who begins a meal with "a *bouillon* the clarity of which announced it had more quantity than quality."

Honoré Daumier, the most gifted and acerbic of France's 19th-century satirists, also dealt with this unglamorous topic. Two of his images captured the importance of *bouillon* in the lives of the poor. The first showed a *Soupe Populaire,* one of the charity kitchens set up to feed the needy. An obese cook contemptuously ladles out soup for two emaciated and bandaged clients who complain of its weakness. Where are the bones that give it nourishment? With straight-faced sarcasm, the cook explains the only bones he could find were domino plaques which, before the arrival of plastics, were carved from bone or ivory. He'd thrown in an additional half set of plaques since the day before, he claims, plus a double six to improve the color.

The second image, called simply *La Soupe* (The Soup), is among Daumier's masterworks. A woman and a man share a wooden table, each hunched over a dish. Indifferent to one another, they spoon up their soup with single-minded need. By showing the woman with a baby at her breast, Daumier emphasizes that soup is the mother's milk of the nation.

Like cheese and wine, soup developed regional variations. *Consommé,* the broth drunk by the gentry, had a refined flavor but little substance, and was intended to stimulate appetite rather than satisfy it. By contrast, *garbure,* a specialty of the Gascon country of the south-west, combined *bouillon* with vegetables and a variety of meats, usually smoked or salted, to create something between soup and stew. In Provence, *pistou,* a paste of pine nuts pounded with cheese, olive oil and basil, was stirred into the soup, while farther south, along the Mediterranean, fishermen improvised *bouillabaisse,* a

Soupe Populaire, Honoré Daumier, 1844

seafood soup, based on a *bouillon* or *fumet* made from
the shells of crabs and shrimp, into which they tossed
any fish too bony or ugly to sell.

To stretch a soup, cooks incorporated bread,
ranging from *croutons,* the small squares of toast
traditionally served with *consommé,* to the thick slices
covered in grilled Gruyère cheese so important an
ingredient of *soupe à l'oignon.* This speciality of Paris's
Les Halles market gave energy to its laborers, known as
forts or strong men, but also appealed to socialites who,
worn out with partying, dropped by in the small hours

La Soupe, Honoré Daumier, 1865

for a reviving bowl at one of the market's all-night cafés.

Soup reached a peak of refinement under the great chefs of the early 20th century, notably Georges Auguste Escoffier. To make his *soupe à l'oignon,* from acquiring the beef bones for the basic *bouillon* to serving the finished soup with its cheese topping still sizzling from the grill, took three days. He proposed the recipe confident that any well-managed restaurant or hotel kitchen would employ a *sous-chef* specifically to prepare *bouillons* of chicken or beef and keep them simmering at the back of the stove. Such a kitchen would have no trouble preparing, for example, his *Consommé Royale,* for which the chef beat some eggs with cream, poured the mixture into molds, poached it until firm, then cut the omelet-like solid into strips. Placing a few of these in a soup bowl with thin slices of chicken breast, mushroom and truffle, he'd ladle hot chicken consommé on top—a soup literally royal, and fit to be served to a crowned head.

CHAPTER 14

AN ARMY RUNS ON ITS STOMACH

Dining with Napoleon Bonaparte

I n *Love and Death*, his 1975 pastiche of Tolstoy's novel *War and Peace*, Woody Allen pokes fun at Napoleon. Even as he takes possession of Moscow, the emperor frets about his heritage. In particular, he dislikes the pastry his cooks intend to call a Napoleon. "It should have more cream between the crust," he complains, "and no raisins! If this pastry is to bear my name, it must be richer; more cream."

The gâteau about which Allen joked, a triple sandwich of crisp puff pastry filled with sweet cream or custard, does exist, but is called a Napoleon only

French soldiers cooking chicken for Napoleon on the day of the Battle of Marengo, from the French weekly magazine *La Cuisine des Familles*

in Anglo-Saxon countries. To the French, it's a *mille-feuille*, the cake of a thousand leaves. Nor does it date from the time of Napoleon. The Neapolitan, a similar pastry, had already existed for a century. The only foodstuff specifically named for Napoleon is a grade of brandy. Known as XO (extra old), the term designates a blend that has been stored for at least 10 years. He was also commemorated during the 1920s by the Napoleon cocktail, a blend of gin with dashes of the bitter *digestif* Fernet-Branca, the *apéritif* Dubonnet and the citrus liqueur Curaçao.

Although he famously said "an army marches on its stomach," Napoleon had little time for food. Trained as a soldier, he looked on food as fuel, not fun. From paintings and the memoirs of his intimates, we know he was far from the ideal dinner companion. He often arrived at the table late, and ate quickly, racing through a meal in 15 minutes, grabbing whatever was closest. If that happened to be a dessert, he consumed it even before the soup. "Everything ends up in the same place," he said.

Meals were further complicated by his habit of arbitrarily rotating members of his inner circle in and out of favor. A favorite of one week would, for no obvious reason, seem to irritate him the next, while another won his approval, until that person in turn also lost his confidence. The technique, which kept his intimates off balance, competing to please him, didn't improve their digestion.

Napoleon's chronic gastritis dictated dishes without spice or rich sauces.

He preferred potatoes, beans and lots of bread, which he dunked in soup or used to mop up gravy. Anxious to satisfy his every whim, his cooks served a range of dishes, hoping one would tempt him. According to one of his valets, breakfast, the most important meal of the day, could include "boiled or poached eggs, an omelette, a small leg of mutton, a cutlet, a filet of beef, broiled breast of lamb, or a chicken wing, lentils, [or] beans in a salad."

Dinner was more elaborate, the table more abundantly served, but he never ate any but the most simply cooked things. A piece of Parmesan or Roquefort cheese closed his meals. If there happened to be any fruit, it was served to him, but if he ate any of it, it was but very little. For instance, he would only take a quarter of a pear or an apple, or a very small bunch of grapes. What he especially liked were fresh almonds. He was so fond of them that he would eat almost the whole plate.

His cooks, of which he used up 11 in the course of his military career, struggled to create dishes suited to his delicate stomach. According to legend, after the battle of Marengo on June 14, 1800, at which the young Napoleon defeated the forces of Italy, his chef, Dunand, searched nearby houses for fresh ingredients. Finding a small chicken, some freshwater crayfish, mushrooms, eggs, garlic and tomatoes, he cut up the chicken, sautéed it with garlic, added tomatoes and mushrooms, and garnished the dish with fried eggs. Enthusiastically received by Napoleon, "Chicken

Marengo" became a regular feature at his table, and, in the eyes of the emperor, a lucky one. When, on one occasion, Dunand omitted the crayfish, the emperor protested, "You will bring me bad luck!"

Like many tales about Napoleon, this one has been debunked. Dunand was in Russia at the time of Marengo and didn't join the Imperial staff until 1801, nor did he record details of this recipe until 1809. Napoleon's dinner on the night after Marengo was not cooked by Dunand. Instead, the Emperor, hearing that one of his marshals, François-Étienne Kellermann, was about to enjoy a meal provided by a monastery, sent his cook to commandeer it.

Satirists attacking the ruling classes in France often did so in terms of food. Louis XVI was parodied for his gluttony, while Napoleon's greed for territory gave British cartoonist James Gillray the idea for the 1805 cartoon known as *The Plumb-pudding in Danger or State Epicures Taking un Petit Souper*. When the British prime minister, William Pitt, was rumored to be considering a treaty with Napoleon, Gillray showed the two leaders at table, dividing the globe like a pudding, with Pitt getting the oceans and Napoleon the land.

Napoleon may not have enjoyed eating but he understood food's seductive power. In 1804, he asked his closest adviser, Charles-Maurice de Talleyrand, to transform his family chateau of Valençay into a country retreat for high-level political meetings. A true gourmet, Talleyrand, famous for his comment, "Show me another pleasure like dinner which comes every day and lasts an hour," chose as his chef the famous

The Plumb-pudding in Danger or State Epicures Taking un Petit Souper,
James Gillray

pâtissier Marie-Antoine Carême, but first set him a
test: Create a year of menus, never repeating a dish,
and using only seasonal produce. Carême succeeded
with ease.

News of Napoleon's disastrous 1812 invasion of
Russia appalled Carême. "One hundred thousand men
dead," he said, "*and 50 chefs!*" Many members of the
various noble households were friends, among them
Laguipierre, chef of the Élysée Palace, who froze to
death during the retreat.

Talleyrand foresaw the emperor's downfall, and
planned accordingly. As Czar Alexander I rode into
Paris after Waterloo, he was cheered as the savior of
France. While his troops pitched their tents under the

trees of the Champs-Élysées, he wondered where to make his headquarters, particularly since it wasn't clear who was to be the new head of state. His advisers favored the Élysée Palace, Napoleon's former residence, until an anonymous note arrived, warning that the building was mined with explosives.

At the same time, Talleyrand invited Alexander to enjoy the hospitality of his home, not to mention the pleasures of his table. The czar accepted, and was so impressed by the food that, when he returned to St. Petersburg, he offered Carême the choice of becoming *maître d'* to his household or his head chef. As for the note, it was found to be a hoax—with either Talleyrand or Carême suspected as the culprit.

In Woody Allen's *Love and Death*, Napoleon is also worried about competition: "My spies tell me that my illustrious British enemy is working on a new meat recipe he means to call Beef Wellington." Though one of his cooks sneers, "It will never get off the ground," Beef Wellington, also known as *boeuf en croûte*, a filet of beef baked in a pastry crust, did become a staple of *haute cuisine,* but not for any reason connected with the Duke of Wellington. Of the stories circulating about the source of this dish, the most credible links it not to the victor of Waterloo but to the city of Wellington in New Zealand.

The same Wellington claims credit for another celebrity dish, the dessert known as the Pavlova. Supposedly created to celebrate the Russian ballerina's 1926 tour of Australasia, this shell of meringue filled with whipped cream and fruit belongs to a tradition of desserts inspired by divas. In 1893, when

Australian soprano Nellie Melba worried that the
ice cream she enjoyed might chill her vocal cords,
master chef Escoffier, who had already accommodated
her wish for a light crispbread by inventing Melba
Toast, created Pêche Melba, which insulated scoops
of vanilla ice cream in a pink-tinted syrup that made
them resemble peaches. Less warmly remembered is
the Marlene, a concoction of blue ice cream inspired
by Marlene Dietrich's most famous film *The Blue
Angel.* During her 1968 Australian tour, the chef at
a Sydney hotel chose to unveil his creation at a press
conference. Marlene placed it on the floor by her
chair where it melted, unsampled. It has not been
heard of since.

Military men and their victories are frequently
celebrated in food. When Marshal Ferdinand Foch,
Supreme Commander of French forces during
World War I, visited New Orleans in 1919, the
city's foremost restaurant, Antoine's, created Oysters
Foch. As damaging to the digestion as any bayonet,
it consisted of oysters breaded with cornmeal, deep-
fried, served on toast smeared with *foie gras,* the entire
dish doused in the buttery, tarragon-flavored Sauce
Colbert. Three decades later, when the grandiose
Field Marshal Bernard Montgomery announced that
he preferred to go into battle only when his troops
outnumbered the enemy 17 to one, Ernest Hemingway
persuaded Paris's Ritz Hotel bar to serve the no-less-
disastrous Montgomery Martini, made with one part
of vermouth to 17 of gin.

Among dishes created for military celebrities, few
compare with that named for André Malraux. Novelist,

filmmaker, convicted plunderer of Cambodian tombs, he became a leader of the resistance during World War II. Not one to let the Germans interfere with his social life nor his pursuit of pleasure, he regularly visited Nazi-occupied Paris to dine with his mistress, the writer Louise de Vilmorin, at Fouquet's on the Champs-Élysees, or at Lasserre, where proprietor René Lasserre prepared his favorite dish: a whole pigeon, deboned, stuffed with *foie gras* and wild mushrooms, briefly roasted with *vin jaune* and truffle juice, and served with baby onions, carrots, beets, turnips and pear on a bed of lettuce, dressed with a reduction of the cooking juices mixed with Madeira. The fame of this dish spread as far as Washington, D.C. After dining with Richard Nixon at the White House in 1972, Malraux told Lasserre, "Consider yourself flattered, my friend. As we began dinner, Nixon smiled and said, *'Monsieur le Ministre*, I don't claim our kitchen is the equal of Lasserre but we will do our best.'"

After the war, Malraux locked horns with another alpha male, Ernest Hemingway. Visiting the writer in his suite at the Ritz, where he was holding court after a lightning dash from the Channel coast just after D-Day, Malraux asked how many men he had commanded in the field. When Hemingway ducked the question—the Geneva Convention forbade war correspondents taking part in hostilities—Malraux informed him he had led a brigade, then demanded how many men Hemingway had actually killed. At this, one of the guerrillas of his retinue drew him aside. "Listen, Papa," he whispered, "do you want

me to shoot this asshole?" Fortunately, Malraux was
spared to become Minister of Culture under General
de Gaulle.

CHAPTER 15

ABSINTHE, THE GREEN FAIRY

"You see things as they really are."—Oscar Wilde

"After the first glass of absinthe," wrote Oscar Wilde, "you see things as you wish they were. After the second, you see them as they are not. Finally you see things as they really are, and that is the most horrible thing in the world."

As Orson Welles remarked in the film *The Third Man,* Switzerland's contributions to European culture begin and end with the cuckoo clock. Absinthe is a partial exception. The 18th-century Swiss distillers who

The Absinthe Drinker, Viktor Oliva, 1901

flavored alcohol with anise, fennel and the bitter herb
Artemisia absinthium—wormwood—may not have
expected this pale green brew with the taste of licorice
to appeal so powerfully to their French neighbors. They
would, however, have known that pastilles of salted
licorice—*réglisse*—were a popular French aid to digestion:
something Anglo-Saxons found difficult to believe, raised
as they were on licorice as confectionery: slick black
straps of the stuff, called Liquorice Whips, or gaudily
tinted cubical sweets known as Liquorice All-Sorts.

Unlike the candy, absinthe was not for children.
With an alcohol level approximately double that of
whiskey, the "hard stuff" didn't come much harder. Even
the traditional method of imbibing absinthe, trickling
ice water through a cube of sugar into the spirit, didn't
dilute it much, since serious drinkers stopped the
moment its color changed to a cloudy beige. Others
drank it neat, relishing the translucent pale green that
earned it the name *La Fée Verte* (The Green Fairy).

Through the late 19th century and into the early
part of the 20th, absinthe was the preferred tipple of
bohemian France. Drunk in moderation, it was no
more dangerous than whiskey or brandy, unless, as was
occasionally the case, a careless distiller failed to extract
all the thujone, the alkaloid that gave it that special
kick—at the cost, however, of one's health. Even as he
refilled his glass, the poet Paul Verlaine, an absinthe
addict, cursed "this horrible drink, the source of folly and
crime, of idiocy and shame, which governments should
tax heavily if they do not suppress it altogether."

The risks didn't deter Ernest Hemingway, James
Joyce, Edgar Degas, Amedeo Modigliani, Pablo Picasso,

L'Absinthe, Edgar Degas, 1875-76, Musée d'Orsay

The Green Muse, Albert Maignan, 1895, Musée de Picardie d'Amiens

Vincent van Gogh, Marcel Proust and Erik Satie, all of whom indulged. Charles Baudelaire included it among the "artificial paradises" of his poem cycle *Les Fleurs du mal* (Flowers of Evil). Henri de Toulouse-Lautrec, who often carried a supply in the glass tube hidden in his cane, drank it in a potent cocktail called *Tremblement de terre* (Earthquake), which mixed absinthe with cognac, to devastating effect. (The same ingredients, with the addition of a cube of sugar and a dash of bitters, make up the Sazerac, most associated with the city of New Orleans.)

Many painters, including Picasso, Manet and Toulouse-Lautrec, documented the effects of inferior absinthe or excessive imbibing. Like Edgar Degas' *Absinthe*, a painting of a couple sitting numbed in a café, they often captured the affectless daze and general untidiness associated with addiction. (Even so, Degas later admitted, to his embarrassment, that, unable to find two suitably degraded addicts, he hired actors to pose.) Lesser artists were not so apologetic about surrendering to melodrama. In Albert Maignan's 1895 *The Green Muse*, a poet is lured from his desk by the fairy herself, who places her hands over his eyes, filling his mind with thoughts of the nearest bar. Viktor Oliva's 1901 *The Absinthe Drinker* shows the fairy, naked, perched on the restaurant table of an inebriated gentleman while a waiter hovers in the distance, wondering why his client is acting so strangely.

In 1914, alarmed by the national rise in alcoholism, the French government banned absinthe on the pretext that it sapped the will of young men of military age, making them disinclined to leave the

Paul Verlaine, portrait in front of a glass of absinthe at the Café Procope, Paris

trenches and walk into the fire of German machine guns. (Conveniently forgotten was the fact that the army had once issued absinthe to troops as a possible protection from malaria.) Stigmatized as the bad boy of booze, absinthe was attacked by journalists in tirades that verged on the hysterical. "Absinthe makes you crazy and criminal," claimed one wildly inaccurate report, "provokes epilepsy and tuberculosis, and has killed thousands of French people. It makes a ferocious beast of man, a martyr of woman, and a degenerate of the infant, disorganizes and ruins the family and menaces the future of the country."

For half a century, absinthe hovered in a limbo
of fantasy and speculation. Distillers ceased production.
Stocks in hotels and restaurant cellars dwindled
until only a few authentic pre-1914 bottles survived.
Enthusiasts made do with Pastis and Pernod, flavored
with licorice and anise. After World War II, researchers
used the few bottles unearthed from forgotten caves to
analyze the content and recreate the formula, and the
green fairy once again floated above the cafés and bars of
Paris. The stigma remained, however. A 1970 exhibition
in the Jeu de Paume hung Degas's painting next to a
photograph of a numbed Paul Verlaine seated with a glass
of absinthe before him.

CHAPTER 16

THE IMPORTANCE OF BREAD

Jean-François Millet's The Gleaners

No food embodies such a complex symbolic meaning as bread. Since biblical times, it has represented the irreducible minimum required for survival. For millenia, the price and quality of the basic loaf provided a barometer of a nation's health, while a citizen's social and cultural level was measured by the kind of bread he or she ate. In France, "to eat one's white bread first" signified someone who achieved early success, only to fail in later life, while there was no greater praise

The Gleaners, Jean-François Millet, 1857, Musée d'Orsay

than to call a person, *"Bon, comme le bon pain"* ("Good, like good bread").

Bread's artistic significance to the French was further confirmed in 2015 when the notebooks of Marcel Proust revealed that the inspiration of *À la recherche du temps perdu* was not, as in the first volume, *Du côté de chez Swann,* a fragment of madeleine, dissolved in a few drops of his aunt's lime flower tisane. Rather, according to the literary scholar who unraveled Proust's spidery annotations, the author, as he writes that passage, "has not still definitively chosen the cake 'shaped by the mold in the form of Saint Jacques's shell.' He hesitates, envisages various types of pastry, a slice of *pain grillé,* even considers a cookie. It's not until his mother enters the story that he decides at last on the archetypal Proustian madeleine." Who knows what different directions this masterpiece might have taken had he not selected the madeleine but gone ahead with his first idea, a humble slice of slightly burned *pain grillé*: i.e., toast.

One of the few artists to treat bread and grain with the respect they deserved was Jean-François Millet. The most emblematic of his works, *Les Glaneuses* (The Gleaners), painted in 1857, shows three peasant women combing a field for stalks of wheat left behind by the harvest. (Exceptionally in France, the right to glean is guaranteed by law, a concession granted by Henry IV in 1554, but limited to the day following a harvest). After picking over the fields, the gleaners moved to the threshing floor, where grain was winnowed from chaff. As a boy, Henri Matisse rescued any grain that lodged in the grooves between tiles. For every 20 grams he retrieved, his father paid him the smallest coin then in use, a sou.

Poet Frédéric Mistral, the child of Norman farmers, grew up surrounded by images of sowing, reaping and gleaning. As an adult, he moved south to Arles in Provence, where he remembered "troops of gleaners who traveled all over the region. They slept in the fields under little tents to protect themselves against mosquitoes, and a third of their gleaning went to the hospital, according to the custom of Arles." Work in the fields demanded a robust diet:

> *The reapers had five meals a day. At 7 o'clock, breakfast: a pickled anchovy, spread on a slice of bread dipped in vinegar and oil, and a very hot red onion; about 10 o'clock the 'Big Drink,' consisting of a hard boiled egg in its shell with a chunk of cheese; at one o'clock, dinner, made up of soup and boiled vegetables; about four o'clock 'tea,' a big salad with a 'capon' of bread rubbed with garlic, and in the evening, supper; pork or lamb, or a so-called 'harvester' omelette, with onions.*

After failing as a portrait painter, Millet was inspired by Honoré Daumier's pictures of the urban poor to apply the same searching examination to the peasantry. This was dangerously out of step with the art establishment of the time. Hoping to repair the image of the government and the church, the authorities encouraged "history paintings" that celebrated military triumphs and stories from mythology and the Bible. These received preferential hanging at the annual salons, and their artists were first in line for lucrative commissions to decorate public buildings or serve on influential committees.

Critics and fellow artists derided Millet's canvases of a sower scattering seed, a woman baking bread and farm workers gathering the potato harvest. In particular, they disliked *Les Glaneuses.* Millet worked on the painting for 10 years. The three women represent the three stages of this backbreaking work, one scanning the ground, another bending down, the third straightening up. The size of the canvas, approximately a meter square, challenged the worth of history paintings by depicting peasant life in the dimensions normally devoted to figures of the great. Critics also protested the picture's political subtext, which contrasts the stoop labor of the gleaners in the foreground with the prosperity of the farm-owners, represented by the haystacks and piled stooks of wheat in the distance, and the mounted steward, ensuring the women move on at sunset.

Les Glaneuses sold for far less than Millet hoped, so he welcomed a commission from the American poet and sometime patron of the arts, Thomas Gold Appleton, for his next major work, the image of a peasant couple, heads bowed, praying for the success of the potato crop. When Appleton failed to collect the painting, Millet added a church steeple in the background and retitled it *The Angelus,* implying that the man and woman have paused for the prayer of that name, traditionally offered at 6 a.m., noon and 6 p.m., and signaled by the tolling of church bells. The painting may even have had an additional secret agenda. In 1933, Spanish Surrealist Salvador Dalí wrote *The Tragic Myth of Millet's Angelus,* an essay suggesting the couple are actually praying over

The Angelus, Jean-François Millet, 1857–1859, Musée d'Orsay

the body of a dead child. Art historians scorned his theory—until the canvas was X-rayed, revealing an over-painted shape at their feet, resembling a coffin.

By the time Millet died in 1875, he was acknowledged as a pioneer of social realism. Lithography had made *The Gleaners* and *The Angelus* a feature of pious parlors and religious institutions all over the world. In 1867, the Exposition Universelle presented a retrospective exhibition, including both canvases. Gleaning remains a feature of French life. More than a century later, filmmaker Agnès Varda made *Les Glaneurs et la glaneuse* (The Gleaners and I), an account of the modern-day scavengers who carry on the practice of gleaning, both in France's fields and orchards, and in the streets of its cities, collecting and recycling discarded objects into art.

CHAPTER 17

EN PLEIN AIR

Lunch in the garden with Claude Monet

Preferring to work *en plein air,* many 19th-century artists moved to the country. The greater the distance from the city, the cheaper it became to buy property and staff it. In 1907, Pierre-Auguste Renoir, crippled with arthritis, bought Les Collettes, a farm at Cagnes-sur-Mer, in the hills above Nice, and had the farmhouse rebuilt to accommodate his problems with movement. As well as a car and chauffeur, he installed an equally rare private phone. A team of servant girls, directed by his wife and former model, Aline, catered to his every wish, preparing his favorite meals, physically

The Lunch, Claude Monet, 1873, Musée d'Orsay

Monet in his dining room decorated with his collection of Japanese wood-block prints

carrying him to a scenic location, then disrobing to pose for him.

At Giverny, 80 kilometers from Paris, Claude Monet established one of the most enduring of artists' environments. After moving there in 1883, he bought the property in 1890, along with a small working farm, and extended it to accommodate his 10-person family. While meticulously planted flower beds demonstrated his theories about color, a Japanese-style garden inspired his studies of *nymphéas* or water lilies that preoccupied him until his death in 1926.

In addition to Marguerite, his cook, Monet employed a gardener, Felix, and a chauffeur/sommelier who drove him as well as managing the wine cellar and maintaining his studio. Additional staff worked the farm, rearing poultry for the table and harvesting the eggs that enriched the Monet diet. Boxes in the kitchen large enough to hold 116 eggs were kept permanently filled.

Monet's day began about 5 a.m., when he breakfasted on cheese, an omelet *aux fines herbes,* sometimes with the addition of cold meat or sausage, accompanied by toast and *confiture*, washed down with tea. With Alice, his wife, he discussed the week's menus, based on seasonal produce. Salads and vegetables came from their own *potager* or vegetable garden. Wild *cèpes* and *girolle* mushrooms, asparagus, fresh herbs and greens such as *roquette* would be foraged from the fields and verges around Giverny.

Monet never entertained at night, going to bed at 9:30, but frequently invited friends to Sunday lunch, which began promptly at 11:30 a.m. In summer, they ate alfresco. Even before he moved to Giverny, Monet celebrated the pleasure of open-air eating in the 1873 painting *Le Déjeuner* (Lunch), an idyllic image of ladies about to sit down at a table set out in shade, with fruit and wine.

In colder weather, they ate in the lemon yellow dining room, its walls hung with some of Monet's collection of Japanese wood-block prints. Monet himself designed the dinner service of a yellow and blue Limoges porcelain, edged in a thick stripe of yellow bordered by a thin line of blue, a pattern that became nationally popular. Guests might include poets Stéphane Mallarmé and Paul Valéry, sculptor Auguste Rodin, painters Paul Cézanne, Henri de Toulouse-Lautrec and James McNeill Whistler.

Monet's dining room at Giverny

The Galette, Claude Monet, 1882

A typical meal began with tomatoes or onions stuffed with a minced meat *farce*, or mushrooms baked with butter under a *gratin* of breadcrumbs. A *gigot* of lamb or a roasted chicken followed. In honor of his adoptive Normandy home, Monet often served cider rather than wine. Though he didn't cook himself—"I have two skills only," he wrote, "horticulture and painting"—the artist, a serious gastronome, kept a diary detailing meals he had enjoyed in his travels. Marguerite attempted to replicate some of them in her blue-tiled kitchen, with varying success. After sampling Yorkshire pudding at the Savoy hotel in London, Monet obtained its recipe for this savory baked batter cake, traditionally served with roast beef, but it never tasted quite the same in France. Marguerite had more success with banana ice cream, which became a regular feature at Monet's table.

Concerned that France's culinary heritage was being eroded, Monet collected recipes for classic dishes. Cézanne, a native of Provence, supplied details of the Mediterranean seafood stew *bouillabaisse*, while Jean-François Millet, painter of *The Gleaners* and other images of the harvest, explained how to make bread rolls. Monet particularly enjoyed the upside-down apple dessert *tarte Tatin*, invented in 1880 by two sisters, Stéphanie and Caroline Tatin. Lacking an oven, they cooked an apple cake on the stove-top, where the heat reacted with butter and sugar to caramelize the fruit. Determined to have the authentic recipe, Monet traveled to the Tatins' home in Lamotte-Beuvron, 160 kilometers south of Paris, to acquire it.

CHAPTER 18

COMFORT FOOD

Henri Matisse's codfish paste and devil's potatoes

J acqueline Duhême was barely 20 when she went to work as assistant to the painter Henri Matisse in 1947. Surgery for abdominal cancer in 1941 had left the artist, then approaching 80, mostly confined to his bed or a wheelchair, but he continued to paint, making use of his immobility to experiment with cutout shapes in colored paper which he incorporated into vivid collages. At the same time, he was completing his last major work, the decoration of the Chapel of the Rosary in the Provençal village of Vence. (Duhême's first job was to pose for the figure of a nun in one of his murals.)

Henri Matisse in the Chapel of the Rosary

Matisse needed help with everything, including meals. Duhême had her baptism by fire when both his son and the painter's companion, Lydia Delectorskaya, were absent for a few days, leaving her in sole charge of the house and staff, including the kitchen. Out of the blue, Matisse asked the cook to prepare some of the dishes he'd eaten as a boy in northern France. The first, *flamiche au poireaux* (leek tart with cream), had been a speciality of his mother. The cook knew that recipe, but was baffled by his next request, for *brandade de morue,* a puree of dried salt cod. Worse, the artist asked that it be accompanied by *patates au diable,* potatoes roasted with garlic, onions and herbs in a clay utensil known as a *diable* or devil.

"I went to Nice in search of a *diable,*" Duhême recalled. "At last, after trying a number of hardware stores, I was successful. The seller assured me they were far from common in the Midi, and he almost never sold one." The cook faced even more problems in preparing the salt cod, which had to be simmered in milk after being soaked for a day in fresh water, frequently changed. (Cooks on river barges towed the fish behind them, while housewives with flush toilets placed it in the cistern, where the water was refreshed each time someone pulled the chain.)

Jacqueline thought both dishes "terrible," but Matisse was delighted, perhaps because he insisted on washing them down with champagne. For dessert, they shared a fresh pineapple, prepared in the manner taught him by Paul Gauguin, who spent much of his life in Tahiti. Under Matisse's direction, Jacqueline made a series of long deep cuts in the skin, then pulled out lozenges of fruit which they ate with sweet Alsatian white wine.

When Jacqueline visited Picasso in his summer home, La Californie, in the hills behind Cannes, he often invited her to stay for lunch. Eaten in the earth-floored kitchen, next to heaps of rusted food cans, and sometimes observed by a wandering goat named Esmeralda, these meals were anything but gourmet occasions. "Invariably it was vegetable soup, with bread and fruit," she wrote. "Once, he searched everywhere for a can of sardines he'd opened. He finally found them in the refrigerator, frozen solid. He did everything that way. It was all a complete mess, nothing like my boss."

Notorious for never paying for café meals, Picasso would respond to the arrival of the bill by dashing off a sketch on the menu or napkin. According to one famous anecdote, he once invited a large group of friends to an expensive Paris seafood restaurant. When the check arrived, he took the skeleton of the fish he'd eaten, placed it on a piece of paper, traced around the bones with two different colored pencils, signed the drawing and presented it to the waiter, aware that his creation was worth many times the cost of the meal.

Matisse made his reputation with paintings involving food. They include *The Dinner Table,* showing a woman putting the finishing touches to a dining table crowded with wine and fruit. He spent a year on this canvas, his first Impressionist work, completed when he was 27. Shown at the 1897 Salon Nationale, it was greeted with hostility. Visitors found the brushwork "blurry," and Matisse's father was so offended that he refused to continue supporting him financially. Matisse returned to the theme in 1908, but in a very different style, with *La desserte rouge* (Harmony in Red),

The Dinner Table, Henri Matisse, 1897

The Dessert: Harmony in Red, Henri Matisse, 1908, Hermitage Museum

a vivid and stylized image of a maid arranging a bowl of fruit.

An even more radical departure, the 1904 *Luxe, calme et volupté* (Luxury, Calm and Pleasure), recorded his impression of a seaside picnic by the Mediterranean at Saint-Tropez. With André Derain, Maurice de Vlaminck, Raoul Dufy, Othon Friesz, Georges Rouault and Georges Braque, Matisse pioneered a flamboyant, highly colored style that angered the art establishment. At annual salons, their work was often banished to side galleries. When the critic Louis Vauxcelles jeered that a sculpture by Donatello in one such gallery seemed to cower from these invaders as from savage animals, the group truculently took to calling itself *Les Fauves* (Wild Beasts).

CHAPTER 19

SETTING MEALS
TO MUSIC

*Paris café life in the operas
of Puccini and Rossini*

C artoonist Jean-Jacques Sempé is a master at
observing the eccentricities of the French. One
of his drawings shows a modern staging of an
opera set in ancient Rome. Performers in togas lounge
around a table sparsely supplied with wine and a little
fruit. "I went to see Lambert last night," grumbles one
chorus member. "He's an extra in *Lucrezia Borgia*. Every
night, it's hors d'oeuvre, entrée, main dish (fish or meat)
with vegetables, and a choice of cheese or dessert."

Paolo Montarsolo as Don Magnifico in a production of Rossini's *La Cenerentola*, c.1972

Lucrezia Borgia, Gaetano Donizetti's tale of medieval homicide, does contain a number of eating and drinking scenes, but might not have been Sempé's ideal choice, since its most famous aria, the drinking song *Il segreto per esser felici* (The Secret to Being Happy), concludes with all five singers dropping dead, poisoned by Lucrezia.

All the same, the intimate relationship of wine, food and music, traditionally one of the closest in the arts, has long been established in France. In medieval times, artisans were sometimes paid in wine, particularly by the church, which monopolized its production. To christen a new organ, workmen and sponsors "drank its health" by filling one of the pipes with wine, an invitation to both faithful and clergy, for the most pious of reasons, to get roaring drunk.

In the 19th century, the musical celebration of good eating and drinking found its apotheosis in grand opera. Italian composers gravitated to Paris, the most cosmopolitan of Europe's capitals. In the new opera house of Napoleon III's empress, Eugenie, the world's largest and best equipped, Puccini, Donizetti and Rossini enjoyed their greatest successes.

Chorus singers were so much in demand in Paris that they took over certain cafés, making it easier for impresarios to find them in an emergency. The second act of Puccini's *La Bohème,* based on Parisian writer Henri Murger's memories of his impecunious days as a student, takes place in such a cafe, the Momus, which used to stand at 19 rue des Prêtres-Saint-Germain-l'Auxerrois. Strolling among the patrons, to the irritation of her new and venerable protector, the

Le café Momus on the right of the image, 1849, Henri Lévis

artist's model Musetta taunts her former lover Marcello
with the waltz *Quando me'n vo'* (When I Walk),
boasting of her beauty, so great that people stop and
stare in the street.

Gioachino Rossini, 1865

Tournedos Rossini

Notwithstanding the fame of *La Bohème,* the composer with the closest ties to Paris and *haute cuisine* was Gioachino Rossini. Born in Pesaro, he moved to Paris in 1824 at the height of his fame, and alternated between Italy and France for the rest of his life. A passionate gourmet, impressively but genially obese, Rossini was vocal in his appreciation of food:

> *Appetite is for the stomach what love is for the heart. The stomach is the conductor, who rules the grand orchestra of our passions, and rouses it to action. The bassoon or the piccolo, grumbling its discontent or shrilling its longing, personify the empty stomach for me. The stomach, replete, on the other hand, is the triangle of enjoyment or the kettledrum of joy. As for love, I regard her as the prima donna par excellence, the goddess who sings cavatinas to the brain, intoxicates the ear, and delights the heart. Eating, loving, singing and digesting are, in truth, the four acts of the comic opera known as Life, and they pass like the bubbles of a bottle of champagne.*

Rossini's *Falstaff, The Italian Girl in Algiers* and *La Cenerentola* (Cinderella) all contain eating or drinking songs. The massive Falstaff and the character of Don Magnifico in *Cenerentola* both celebrate their love of eating, but the composer's greatest appreciation of food took place offstage. Friendly with the leading chefs of the day, in particular Marie-Antoine Carême, who called him "the only one who has ever understood me," Rossini inspired them to invent dishes in his name, including a salad, poached eggs, chicken and fillet of sole, all prepared *"alla Rossini."*

In most cases, these dishes were distinguished by the richness of their ingredients. Rossini personally created a risotto based on fat-rich beef marrow, and any dish containing truffles or *foie gras* met with his instant approval. Stuffed into a tube of pasta, these two delicacies made another of his signature dishes, Cannelloni alla Rossini. They also feature in the recipe with which he's most associated, Tournedos Rossini.

To create this challenge to the digestion, a thick slice of beef fillet is sautéed in butter and placed on a piece of fried bread, topped with a slice of *foie gras,* then garnished with truffles and completed with a drizzle of sauce based on Madeira wine. Because it needs the minimum of cooking, the dish was often prepared at the table over an alcohol burner, contributing an additional element of theatricality. There's no agreement over who invented the dish— Carême, Dugléré and Escoffier all claim credit—nor can anyone satisfactorily explain its name. If one anecdote is to be believed, Rossini himself is responsible. Watching the chef prepare the dish at the Café Anglais, he became so intrusive that the cook told him to sit down. Put out, Rossini snapped, "Well then, turn your back" (so I can't see what you're doing)"—in French *"Et alors, tournez le dos."*

Operetta composers in the 20th century picked up the theme of café life made famous by Paris. *The White Horse Inn*, a German comedy romance set in a mountain resort, became a hit in the 1930s, both on stage and screen. The success of Sigmund Romberg's *The*

Student Prince, premiered in 1924, was due largely to a rousing song in which the eponymous hero leads his fellow University of Heidelberg students in a celebration of beer. Jacques Offenbach set his ballet *Gaîté Parisienne* in a 19th-century Paris café. At its climax, cancan dancers burst onstage to the music of a *galop* that was ever afterward associated with this dance. The ultimate café operetta, however, was Franz Lehár's 1905 *The Merry Widow*. Composed and premiered in Vienna, it languished until the libretto was rewritten to feature Paris's café Maxim's and the *cocottes* or party girls who hung out there. Since then, it has racked up an estimated million performances, making it the most popular show in musical history.

CHAPTER 20

THE ZOO IS ON THE MENU

Voisin's Christmas feast of 1870

I t's a myth that every French man and woman appreciates good food and knows how to prepare it. Dine with any middle-class family, and you'll likely be served fatless, flavorless roast veal, with green beans and perhaps potato purée, followed by cheese. Some don't cook at all but buy *boeuf bourguignon, poulet chasseur* or *pâté en croûte* at a *traiteur,* or, even more frequently, purchase them frozen at the upmarket Picard chain. Lately, this practice has spread to restaurants, more than two-thirds of whose dishes are bought pre-prepared.

Vous savez. Fricando ? faudra pas y toucher !...

Oh ! je le reconnaîtrai bien celui-là Mam'z'elle Rose, il est juste de la couleur de vos cheveux

Franco-Prussian War 1870-1871: Siege of Paris. Chef trying to reassure woman that he was not suggesting cooking her pet. From *Paris Bloque*, 1871

Traditional cuisine is more common outside the cities, where the virtues of invention, tradition and frugality survive. The point was illustrated by the experience of a family in the country that, having lost its money, decided to economize by firing the cook.

"We're terribly sorry," the wife explained. "It's just that food has become so expensive."

"But Madame," said the cook, relieved she wasn't being dismissed for incompetence, "you should have told me! Give me a few weeks. I can save at least enough money from the housekeeping to pay my wages."

She began by ignoring the best fruit and vegetables at the market. Bruised fruit and over-ripe tomatoes were cheaper, and sometimes could be had for nothing. Squashy tomatoes were perfect for sauces and the damaged fruit for pies. On the way home, she scanned the roadside for snails, and picked roquette, dandelion, marjoram, chives and mint. The greens went into salads, their stalks into stocks and soups, while anything left over was dried to use later.

At the butcher, she chose cheaper cuts, better stewed or braised than roasted. She also insisted that the butcher wrap the bones and trimmings, and add anything his less-frugal clients left behind. ("For the cat," she told him, though nobody was fooled.) Bones and scraps were roasted for the fat, then boiled to make stock for soups. Suet, the hard white fat from around lambs' kidneys, was minced raw, and used to enrich pastry and puddings.

A chicken became a challenge: What part of it *couldn't* be used? By pounding the breast meat into *paillards*, stewing the legs, thighs and wings in red wine for *coq au vin*, and using the bones for soup, a bird could be stretched for three meals, where, as roasted, it did for only one. The liver was reserved for a terrine, and the heart and other edible organs boiled in stock, then "potted" in the skimmed fat. Called *gésiers,* these meaty lumps made a tasty addition to salads. So did the tender "oysters" on either side of the backbone. There's a sneer of peasant superiority in the traditional name for these nuggets: *sot-l'y-laisse*—literally "the stupid leave them."

What else did the stupid leave? Quite a lot. The country housekeeper used almost every part of an animal, including liver, kidney, brains, bones and tongue. *Os à moelle*—veal shinbones—were sawn into rounds, baked, and the marrow spooned onto toast and sprinkled with *fleur de sel,* the dust-fine "flower of the salt" skimmed from the topmost layer of the pans where seawater evaporated. *Ris de veau* or sweetbreads, the sheep's thymus gland, became a gourmet dish when sautéed with walnuts. So was a whole veal kidney in mustard sauce. Tripe, the stomach lining of a cow, could be cooked Normandy-style in a meat sauce and served in a metal dish over burning coals as *tripe à la Caen,* or marinated, stewed, then breaded and fried, in the Lyonnais manner, as *tablier de sapeur*—Sapper's Apron. (Sappers, the military engineers who tunneled under enemy fortifications to plant explosives, wore aprons of cowhide as thick as the slabs of tripe used in this dish.)

Admittedly, there are some things even the French won't eat. The Romans cooked dormice with honey and poppy seeds, but while French fields swarmed with these little rascals, no restaurateur was tempted. In hard times, however, old rules no longer apply. For one period in 1870 and 1871, even wealthy Parisians would have relished a fat dormouse. They *did* devour rat, cat, yak, bear and elephant. What drove them to this extreme? And how did chefs make such animals edible? The answers constitute one of the most curious stories in the history of cookery.

In July 1870, a festering rivalry between Emperor Napoleon III and the kingdom of Prussia erupted into war. Disastrously for France, the emperor, nephew of Napoleon Bonaparte, inherited none of his uncle's military genius. The army of Prussia, efficiently commanded and well-armed, overran the French in their first battle, and took Napoleon prisoner. While they haggled over the terms of surrender, the Prussians besieged Paris.

The siege lasted five months, during which no person or animal could enter or leave the city. For a while, the army sent messages by homing pigeons, until the Prussians imported hawks to intercept them. A greater threat to the birds came from hungry Parisians. As beef, chicken and lamb disappeared, the government, ignoring the decree of Pope Gregory III, urged Parisians to eat horse. By chance, *boucheries chevalines*—horse butchers—had appeared for the first time in France just a few years before, identified, then as now, by a gilded horse's head. Parisians ate 70,000 horses during the siege. At the central market, an entire pavilion was devoted to horse meat. Even the emperor succumbed. Two thoroughbreds, a gift from Czar Alexander II, provided a number of meals for the imperial court.

Once all the horses were used up, it was the turn of Paris's estimated 25,000 cats, followed by dogs, then rats. Their meat was lean, and a little tasteless,

Rats à deux francs (The Rat Butcher), Narcisse Chaillou, 1871

but perfectly edible if well-seasoned. The poor already considered it a delicacy, as did sailors, who fattened rats with biscuit crumbs as an alternative to salt pork and beef. Rat sellers set up in the streets. The painter Narcisse Chaillou, known for sacccharine landscapes and scenes of peasant life, created his most famous canvas when he painted such a young merchant in *Rats à deux francs* in 1871. Cheekily dressed as a chef, down to the apron and toque, the boy is ready to skin the animal and joint its body to order. (Two francs for a rat was by no means cheap; it represented the daily pay of two soldiers.)

No restaurant worked more strenuously to maintain standards than Voisin's. Though the lace-curtained windows of the little establishment at 261 rue St.-Honoré suggested a simple café, its food and wine were famous, and famously expensive. Its waiters included César Ritz, later the business partner of chef Georges-Auguste Escoffier and manager of London's Savoy Hotel, then of the Paris establishment that still bears his name.

Voisin's chef in 1870 was 32-year-old Alexandre Étienne Choron. He knew his discriminating clientele would expect something better than dog, cat or rat. In December, his patience was rewarded when Paris's zoo, the Jardin d'Acclimatation, announced it could no longer feed its animals, and reluctantly offered them for sale as livestock.

Butchers snapped up deer, antelopes and even bear, since all were known to be edible. Imaginatively, M. Debos of the Boucherie Anglaise on boulevard Haussmann bought a yak. Under all that hair, it was, after all, just a kind of buffalo, and could pass for beef. At the end of December, he also paid 27,000 francs for two elephants, Castor and Pollux. Not sure how to slaughter them, he hired a marksman named De Vismes to shoot them from 10 meters away with 33mm steel-tipped explosive bullets.

The Boucherie Anglaise became news. A cartoonist drew an imaginary scene inside Debos's shop. Backed by hooks from which dangle giant legs of elephant and the heads of stags and lions, butchers peel the skin from elephants and ostriches.

By then, Paris's gourmet community was alive with discussion about the relative edibility of various

Engraving of horse-meat market

animals. American writer Nathan Sheppard reported eating jugged cat with mushrooms, mice on toast, roast donkey and potatoes, and rats cooked with peas and celery. "It would be difficult," he added, "to take a restaurant meal now in Paris without being served one of these animals." Adolphe Michel, editor of the newspaper *Le Siècle,* ate dog cutlets with green peas and kebabs of dog liver. The cutlets were over-marinated, he noted, but the kebabs were "tender and completely agreeable."

American journalist Thomas Gibson Bowles boasted of eating camel, antelope, dog, donkey, mule and elephant, of which he liked elephant the least. Another commentator, Henry Labouchère, reported,

"Yesterday, I had a slice of Pollux for dinner. It was tough, coarse and oily. I do not recommend English families to eat elephant as long as they can get beef or mutton." He probably ate inferior meat from the torso of the elephant, which Debos sold for 10 to 14 francs a pound. More discriminating chefs, including Choron, bought the tender trunks at three or four times that price.

Some animals defied even Choron's expertise. A hippopotamus at 80,000 francs found no takers. Who knew if the blubbery beast was even edible? Lions and tigers were also left alone. Nobody wanted the job of killing them. But elephant, bear, camel, kangaroo, antelope, wolf, cat and rat all figured in a legendary midnight Christmas dinner offered by Voisin's in December 1870. This is the menu:

Butter, radishes, stuffed Donkey's head, Sardines.
Puree of Red Beans with croutons.
Consommé d'Elephant.
Fried baby Catfish.
Roasted Camel English style.
Kangaroo Stew
Bear chops with pepper sauce.
Haunch of Wolf with Venison sauce.
Cat, flanked by Rats.
Watercress salad.
Antelope Terrine with truffles.
Cèpes mushrooms Bordelaise style.
Green peas with butter.
Rice pudding with preserves.
Gruyère cheese.

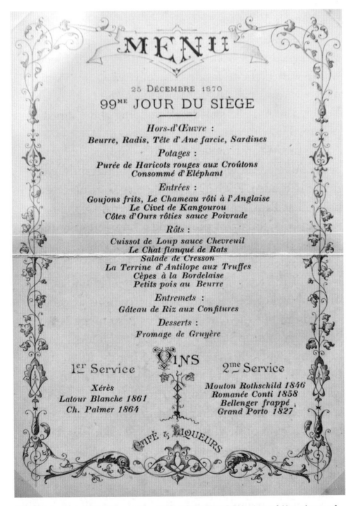

Voisin's menu dated December 28, 1870, the 99th day of the siege of
Paris by the Prussian army

The banquet, meant as a one-off demonstration of Choron's skill, backfired as clients developed a taste for elephant. After Christmas, Voisin's bought the animal of the Botanical Garden or Jardin des Plantes for 15 francs a pound. Elephant trunk in *sauce chasseur* and *Éléphant bourguignon* went back on the menu. Even the blood wasn't wasted. Edmond de Goncourt wrote in his diary on New Year's Eve 1870, "Tonight, at the famous Chez Voisin, I found elephant black pudding and I dined"—presumably with pleasure.

The Voisin banquet was not simply a culinary event but a social and political one. Significantly, the menu is headed "99th Day of the Siege." It made the point that Paris remained defiant. Given that the meal was, in part, an act of propaganda, how seriously should we take the menu?

Some dishes sound authentic. A stew of kangaroo is one of the few ways to eat this muscular animal. The tail makes a tasty soup and the rump is as good as venison, but the remaining meat is so tough it's usually ground up for pet food. Rat is still a delicacy in China, where it was sampled during the 1990s by British TV chef Keith Floyd. He found it "not in any way repugnant. It tasted similar to duck." Floyd, who specialized in exotic dishes eaten in remote places, also roasted a *gigot* of bear. It tasted, Floyd said, like the best roast pork. Choron probably followed a similar recipe, larding the meat with slivers of bacon and inserting pieces of garlic.

Of the menu's other dishes, not even Floyd would have suggested roasting the notoriously tough camel, or serving wolf at all. One must also be suspicious of

Stuffed Donkey's Head. As a donkey's head has little edible meat, it's probable the head was decorative; something in *papier-mâché,* borrowed from a theatrical warehouse that kept it in stock for productions of *A Midsummer Night's Dream.* Cat Flanked by Rats also sounds suspicious. No chef would place such an unappetizing oddity next to Antelope Terrine with Truffles, clearly a dish of distinction. On the other hand, it would not be beyond the skill of Voisin's kitchen to create a cat and rats in aspic, or in shortcrust, enclosing a *pâté en croûte.*

To have staged such a patriotic event made Voisin's more famous than ever. It even opened a branch in New York. Until the original closed in 1930, customers included kings and princes, as well as the great of politics and the arts. It no longer served elephant and camel, but "if the owner looks upon you with eyes of favor," wrote one client, "you will be presented by him with a little pink card, folded in two, on which is the menu of a dinner given at Voisin's on Christmas Day 1870."

CHAPTER 21

ON THE FRENCH RIVIERA

Renoir, Colette, Picasso, Fitzgerald and Hemingway enjoy the flavors of the Côte d'Azur

F ew events had so far-reaching an influence on French cultural life as the development of the Mediterranean Riviera. Throughout the 19th century, the towns of Nice, Cannes, Antibes, Hyères, Saint-Tropez, Menton and Monte Carlo were largely inaccessible except by sea. Russian aristocrats, who spoke French among themselves and regarded France as their

Promenade de la Croisette in Cannes, c.1880

Queen Victoria at breakfast with princesses in Nice, 1895

spiritual home, flocked to the Côte d'Azur as soon
as the northern rivers froze in October and remained
there until May, often joined by members of the British
and German nobility, with whom they shared a blood
relationship. As Guy de Maupassant, visiting Cannes,
noted in 1888, "Princes, princes, everywhere princes!
Those who love princes are indeed happy. No sooner had
I set foot yesterday morning on the promenade of the
Croisette than I met three, one after another."

Many visitors to the Riviera were invalids, hoping the hot dry climate would relieve the symptoms of their diseases, in particular tuberculosis. In 1907, Pierre-Auguste Renoir, almost paralyzed by arthritis, bought Les Collettes, a hilltop farm at Cagnes-sur-Mer. Amid its giant olive trees and orange groves, and bathed in near-tropical heat, he was able to continue painting for another 20 years. Marc Chagall and Henri Matisse followed, Pierre Bonnard made his home at Le Cannet, while an artists' colony sprang up in Saint-Tropez around Paul Signac.

Traditionally, foreigners returned home in May, leaving the coast to fishermen and a handful of artists attracted by the Mediterranean light and heat. Composer Cole Porter and his wife, Linda, were the first Americans to ignore the "season" and spend all summer on the Riviera. In 1921 and 1922, they rented a villa near Antibes. Gerald Murphy, proprietor of the Mark Cross luxury leather goods stores and Porter's best friend at university, visited them with his wife, Sara, and subsequently bought a house in Antibes, which they called Villa America. Their guests over the next decade included Scott and Zelda Fitzgerald, Pablo Picasso, Man Ray, John Dos Passos, Dorothy Parker, Jean Cocteau, and Ernest and Hadley Hemingway—followed not long after by Hadley's successor, Pauline Pfeiffer.

The Murphys and their way of life inspired Scott Fitzgerald's last completed novel, *Tender Is the Night*. Though the book describes dinner conversation among these privileged individuals, the clothes they wore and, naturally, the booze they drank—generally Veuve Clicquot champagne—it seldom mentions food.

Whatever the reason for Anglo-Saxons visiting the Côte d'Azur, it wasn't to eat.

How to Be Happy on the Riviera, a British guide of 1927, devotes most of its chapters on food to warnings about larcenous restaurateurs who padded *l'addition* and served dishes that were never ordered. If food is mentioned, it's usually to disparage it. "Too much butter is used," it says of Provençal cuisine in general. "Too many dishes which would otherwise be palatable [are] spoiled by highly flavored sauces." Beef is "on the tough side," mutton is "awful," white asparagus "bitter" and other boiled vegetables "a ghastly job." As for seafood, it calls fried fresh sardines "rather a disappointment. There can be no doubt that Providence intended sardines to be tinned." While cautiously approving local wines, particularly rosé, it warns that the Anglo-Saxon palate may find them "acidic," in which case "an excellent corrective is to add a little hot water, a tablespoon to a glass being sufficient."

The French reaction could not have been more different. The novelist Colette, who lived in Saint-Tropez for many years and was described by the correspondent of *The New Yorker* magazine, Janet Flanner, as "an artistic gourmet in a country where eating ranks as an art," embraced the local cuisine, particularly its fiery garlic. (*How to Be Happy on the Riviera* fails even to mention this indispensable ingredient of Provençal food.) Most meals *chez* Colette began, according to her husband Maurice Goudeket, with

> *a crust of bread dipped in olive oil, lavishly rubbed in garlic and sprinkled with coarse salt. Cooked garlic*

Picking up olives in Alpes-Maritimes, c. 1900

seasoned every dish and in addition, throughout the whole meal, Colette ate raw cloves of it as if they had been almonds. Lunch consisted of Provençal dishes only: green melons, anchoiade [anchovies pounded with garlic, oil and vinegar, and served as a dip with raw vegetables], *stuffed rascasse, rice with favouilles* [small green crabs], *bouillabaisse and aioli* [garlic mayonnaise].

Provençal produce was legendary. "There are gardens of beans, orchards with apples, pears and peaches," wrote the poet Frédéric Mistral, "cherry trees that catch your eye, fig trees that offer you their ripe fruit, round-bellied melons that beg to be eaten, and beautiful vines with bunches of golden grapes." With so much growing wild, one could eat for nothing. Mistral's school friends habitually played truant, living off the land:

> *The night they spend in piles of straw or in hay-stacks. When hunger comes, they eat wild blackberries, wild plums, almonds left on the tree, or bunches of wild grapes. They eat the fruit of the elm—which they call 'white bread'—onions that have sprouted again, wild beans, beechnuts, and acorns if necessary.*

To celebrate religious or patriotic holidays, French villages often staged fetes featuring local produce. At some, they pelted one another with flowers or the oranges and lemons that grew in profusion on the slopes of the Alpes-Maritimes. More often, they staged the public feasts that had been a feature of medieval village life. Many of these were held to welcome pilgrims walking the long road to the shrines of Saint Joseph of Compostela in Spain. Tables were set up in the town square and a single dish prepared in sufficiently lavish quantities to serve all comers. In Provence, seafood predominated. For a *sardiniarde,* sardines were grilled over wood fires, while for an *aïoli,* slabs of steamed cod or *merlu* (hake) joined boiled potatoes and carrots in celebration of the garlic mayonnaise that gave the event its name.

Towns in Picardy and the north spit-roasted an entire cow or pig. A *boeuf,* roasted *en broche,* fed about 500 people, particularly when served with the traditional

The Village Festival (detail), Jean Charles Meissonier (1815-1891)

accompaniment of *aligot,* a puree of potatoes mixed
with melted cheese in the proportions of two measures
of potatoes to one of cheese, and further enriched with
butter, cream and crushed garlic. Such events were a
popular subject for painters, particularly artists like the
wildly popular Jean-Charles Meissonier, who specialized
in large and busy canvases for the annual salons. His
Le Festival au village (The Village Festival) celebrates an
innocent lifestyle known to few communities. Earlier
artists, among them Peter Paul Rubens, added coded
comments to such scenes, inserting, for example, the
image of a pig, the symbol of bestial excess.

As new railway services increased the flow of newcomers into the Côte d'Azur, restaurateurs arrived from Italy, Sicily and Corsica to feed them. Their menus overwhelmed the more modest local cuisine, just as the demands of tourists debased the festivals of flowers and fruit, which degenerated into parades as hired peasantry perched on floats trundled through the streets of Nice and Cannes, pelting cheering crowds with flowers.

"Provençal" became shorthand for any dish of pasta or seafood with a sauce of tomato, garlic, onions and olive oil. The same ingredients, with a few olives, hard-boiled eggs and anchovies, constituted so-called *salade Niçoise*—salad in the style of Nice. These dishes frequently relied for flavor on the mixture of dried aromatics known as *herbes de Provence*. No two manufacturers of this concoction, the curry powder of French cuisine, agreed on its contents. The traditional recipe called for oregano, savory, thyme and basil, but as rosemary replaced the rarer savory, a peppery thyme-like spice, the mixture came to depend on what the merchant had on the shelf: marjoram, tarragon, sage, bay, fennel seed, lavender, dill weed, chervil, even mint and orange zest—just so long as it assaulted the nose with a herbal tang so pungent that unscrupulous drug dealers passed off *herbes de Provence* to their more gullible clients as cannabis.

Culinary abuses didn't dissuade tourists from visiting the Riviera. In the clothing she designed, Coco Chanel popularized the life lived in the sun and open air that had seduced Renoir, Matisse and Chagall. Pablo Picasso's ceramics celebrated the Phoenician merchants who first brought culture to the Mediterranean. Jean

Cocteau's murals for its churches and villas drew on an even earlier source, the Dionysian myths of antiquity, while the Cannes Film Festival catered to the newest and most seductive of all hallucinations, those of movie stardom. The Côte d'Azur became the collective dreamland of France, a sunny playground where any fantasy might be made real.

CHAPTER 22

SURREAL CANNIBALS

Dalí, Buñuel and cannibal fantasies

P rimates were among the few classes of animals
spared in the Paris zoo massacre in 1870.
Following the publication of Darwin's *On the
Origin of Species* in 1859, the theory of evolution was
gaining acceptance, and some people feared that eating
them verged on cannibalism. Not that cannibalism was
entirely unknown in European society. The bodies of
slaves captured and crucified during the Spartacist revolt
in the first century BC were sold for sausage meat. In

Autumnal Cannibalism, Salvador Dalí, 1936, Tate Modern

the 19th century, British companies paid to excavate old battlefields for the bones of common soldiers who'd been buried anonymously where they fell. These were processed into gelatin and glue, or ground up for animal fodder and fertilizer.

During the siege of 1870–1871, cannibalism was occasionally mentioned as, potentially, the greatest challenge to a chef. As one comic suggested, *"Au sauce Madère/On mangera son Grandpère"* (With a sauce of Madeira/We'll eat his grandfather). One and a half centuries later, the Surrealists, who celebrated all forms of misbehavior, also flirted with the idea, evoking it peripherally in the title of their favorite word game *Cadavres Exquis* (Exquisite Corpses), in which players added phrases to a sentence without knowing what had been written before. The game took its name from an early success, *"Le cadavre exquis boira le vin nouveau"* (The exquisite corpse will drink the new wine).

In 1936, as the Spanish Civil war set faction against faction in a violent settling of old scores, Salvador Dalí painted *Autumnal Cannibalism,* "showing a couple, isolated at a table in an otherwise featureless landscape, politely devouring one another with knife and fork. A similar scene appears in the film *L'Âge d'or* (The Golden Age), for which Dalí collaborated with Luis Buñuel. To the accompaniment of the *Liebestod* from Wagner's *Tristan and Isolde,* actor Gaston Modot gnaws at the hand of co-star Lya Lys. Buñuel tried to achieve the effect by having the actor slobber over an already mutilated hand, but at best it approximates Dalí's vision. When he published his wildly unlikely cookbook *Les Dîners de Gala* in 1973, Dalí collected seafood and egg recipes under the heading *Les Cannibalismes de l'automne* (The Cannibalisms of Autumn).

Some women enjoyed offering themselves for devouring, at least in imagination. Cora Pearl, a *grande horizontale* of the *belle époque,* entertained her admirers in style at her Château de Beauséjour on the Loire. This included having herself, nude except for a few sprigs of parsley, carried in to dinner on a large platter supported on the shoulders of four servants, with the exhortation that the diners "cut into" this tasty dish. In 1959 in Berne, Switzerland, Meret Oppenheim staged a "fertility feast," the *pièce de résistance* a naked girl supine amid fruits, nuts and other symbols of fecundity. Under protest, she substituted a dummy, but not before news of the event reached André Breton, who invited her to restage it for the Exposition Internationale du Surréalisme in Paris.

Shortly after, Georges Bardawil wrote the novel *Aimez-vous les femmes?* (Do You Like Women?), the story of a cannibal cult in modern Paris that uses a vegetarian restaurant as a cover for its anthropophagus activities. In 1964, it was adapted into a film starring Sophie Daumier, who posed memorably naked on a large dish, garnished with discreetly arranged pieces of fruit. British director Peter Greenaway may have had this film in mind in 1989 when he made *The Cook, the Thief, His Wife & Her Lover.* A woman whose gangster husband has murdered her lover persuades the chef at his favorite restaurant to roast the body and serve it to her husband, who is forced to sample it at gunpoint. In his Oscar-winning script for the 1965 film *Darling,* Frederic Raphael wrote a scene, never used, in which the

Scene from *Aimez-vous les femmes?*

protagonist, model Diana Scott (Julie Christie), meets with a consortium of executives who are launching her as a corporate entity. After the deal is signed, they ritually consume her in an effigy made of ice cream.

In Paris literary circles, the name most associated with cannibalism was that of globe-trotting American author William Seabrook. An enthusiast for remote places, Seabrook had lived in Africa and among the voodoo priests of Haiti, the subject of his pioneering 1929 study *The Magic Island*. Moving to Paris, Seabrook pursued an interest in sadomasochism, keeping naked women chained around his house and commissioning Man Ray to photograph them.

In 1930, Seabrook published *Jungle Ways,* a description of his time spent in West Africa living with a cannibal tribe, the Guere. When he expressed interest to his tribal friends in the taste of human flesh, they served him a spicy stew, which, they informed him, straight-faced, contained portions of a slain enemy. Never entirely sure he wasn't the victim of a practical joke, Seabrook determined to find out for sure. Exploiting the elastic morality of bohemian Paris, he acquired a portion of human flesh from a friend in the Sorbonne medical school. Handing it to his cook, he asked her to prepare it in a number of ways, hoping one would resemble what he had eaten in Africa. The results, though not unpalatable, were inconclusive. "The steak was slightly tougher than prime veal," he wrote, "a little stringy, but not too tough or stringy to be agreeably edible. The roast, from which I cut and ate a central slice, was tender, and in color, texture, smell as well as taste, strengthened my certainty that of all the meats we habitually know, veal is the one meat to which this meat is accurately comparable."

Visitors to the Louvre are seldom aware that Théodore Géricault's overpowering *Le Radeau de la Méduse* (The Raft of the Medusa), five meters by seven, records an incident of cannibalism. In 1816, the frigate *Méduse* ran aground off the coast of Senegal. Believing they could easily reach land, the passengers built a raft and squeezed 147 on board for what they assumed would be a brief voyage. Instead, the raft was carried out to sea. Passing boats failed to spot it for 13 days, by which time only 15 were left alive, having survived by eating the dead.

Le Radeau de la Méduse (The Raft of the Medusa), Théodore Géricault, 1818–19, Musée du Louvre

Based on the memories of two survivors, and using live models, wax figures and corpses from the morgue, Géricault recreated the incident in his studio. Exhibited at the salon of 1819, the painting caused a sensation. Critics who felt art should educate and uplift were dismissive. "The goal of painting is to speak to the soul and the eyes," said one, "not to repel." Others believed Géricault had captured the survival instincts that lurked just below the surface of civilized society. As one put it, "Our whole society is aboard the raft of the Méduse."

CHAPTER 23

COFFEE TIME

Sartre, de Beauvoir and Camus at the Café de Flore, Modigliani at the Rotonde and Toulouse-Lautrec at the Rat Mort

The late 19th century was the heyday of the café. Once Baron Haussmann, on orders from Emperor Napoleon III, rebuilt Paris around a new network of boulevards, the middle class, accustomed to going around town on horseback or by carriage to avoid the unpaved streets, took advantage of the wide sidewalks to indulge in *flânerie;* strolling simply for the pleasure of it. Merchants who sold coffee, tea and beer courted this passing trade by putting out tables and serving samples of their product. As these proved more

Jean-Paul Sartre and Simone de Beauvoir at the Café de Flore

The Café, Fernard Lungren, 1882-84, Art Institute of Chicago

lucrative than selling in bulk, the café became a feature
of boulevard life.

A few cafés preceded Haussmann. The Procope,
opposite the old Comédie-Française on rue de l'Ancienne-
Comédie, dated from 1686, and welcomed not only
Voltaire but political firebrands Robespierre, Danton and
Marat as they hatched the revolution of 1789. Opposite
the back door was the printery of revolutionary demagogue
Jean-Paul Marat, while the same alley, the Cour de
Commerce St. André, housed the workshop of harpsichord
maker Tobias Schmidt who built France's first guillotine.

Not all cafés began as talk shops for the *bourgeoisie*.
Some evolved from street vendors like those in the Cour
de Commerce who set up benches to sell coffee, milk,

soup and stew. Coal and wood yards also offered a hot drink to chilled and weary deliverymen. Once such merchants moved indoors, their clientele followed.

Rooming houses seldom had kitchens or lavatories, so tenants went straight to their favorite café where they washed up before taking breakfast at the bar or zinc, named for the metal with which the bar was surfaced. After that, likely as not, they spent most of the day at a table, reading the free newspapers, playing chess or gossiping with friends.

Originally cafés served only coffee and alcoholic beverages. Clients left for a restaurant to eat lunch and dinner, but returned for a *digestif.* The Café de Flore in St. Germain-des-Prés was the favorite of existential philosopher Jean-Paul Sartre, his companion Simone de Beauvoir, their friend Albert Camus and the trio's numerous admirers. "We are completely settled there," Sartre explained. "From nine o'clock in the morning until mid-day, we work, then we eat, and at two o'clock we come back and chat with friends until eight o'clock. After dinner, we see people who have an appointment. That may seem strange to you, but we are at home at the Flore."

One could write to someone "c/o Café _____." If the recipient was a regular, the proprietor placed the letter in a rack by the door to be collected. In *Montparnasse*, the first poem he composed after arriving in Paris in 1921, Ernest Hemingway wrote:

> *A Chinese boy kills himself and is dead.*
> *(they continue to place his mail in the letter rack at the Dôme)*

Café du Dôme, Eugène Atget (1857–1927)

Certain cafés were associated with specific national or cultural groups. In Montparnasse, Americans congregated at the Dôme and Hispanics at the Rotonde. Since private phones were unknown and people changed addresses constantly, professions whose work depended on being available at short notice—musicians, chorus singers, small-part actors, artists' models—each had cafés which functioned as social clubs and hiring halls.

Tourists were often startled by the casual nature of French café life. Strangers spoke to one another without being introduced, and the staff, providing a client ordered the occasional coffee or cognac, turned a blind eye to them using the premises as an office. André Breton, disgusted by the "triviality" of Montparnasse, moved his home and the headquarters of the Surrealist

Pablo Picasso, Moïse Kisling and Paquerette enjoying themselves at café La Rotonde, 1916

movement to Montmartre, only to find café life there much the same, with sex workers and drug dealers accorded the same tolerance as any other profession.

In some cases, the raffish nature of the clientele became an attraction. A 1927 guidebook for Americans urged them to visit the Café de la Paix, one of the largest on the Right Bank:

> It is a great vantage point to watch the promenading tourists, the 'Ladies of the Boulevards,' the real Parisians, the Gigolos, the male Perverts, the taxicabs, the hawkers, the beggars. Old women and old men in rags and tatters picking up discarded cigarette stubs. A great rendezvous. The place to tell your friends to meet you.

At the Rat Mort, Henri de Toulouse-Lautrec, 1899, The Courtauld

The art of the café leaned toward sketching and caricature. The artist Nina Hamnett, fresh off the boat from England in 1910, was startled to be accosted in the Rotonde by a handsome but emaciated Italian who introduced himself as "Modigliani, painter and Jew." Chronically broke, "Modi" sketched anyone who paid him a franc. Henri de Toulouse-Lautrec painted such Montmartre hangouts as the Rat Mort (The Dead Rat) and L'Abbaye de Thélème (The Abbey of Thélème, named for a notorious brothel invented by writer François Rabelais), but the most prolific café artists were cartoonists and illustrators. Joseph Hémard, Paul Iribe, Charles Léandre and their colleagues filled the popular weeklies with those images of café society for which the public appetite was inexhaustible. The Coupole, built in 1927 to accommodate American tourists who wanted a place where they could drink, dine and dance, was particularly attractive to artists, some of whom (none very distinguished) painted the square columns that support the ceiling with its trademark cupola.

CHAPTER 24

SHAKEN BUT NOT STIRRED

Add liquor, jazz and Josephine Baker

"Our epoch," announced Dutch painter Kees van Dongen in 1928, "is the cocktail epoch. Cocktails! They are of all colours. They contain something of everything. The modern society woman is a cocktail. Society itself is a bright mixture. You can blend people of all tastes and classes."

Most Parisians didn't agree. Until tourists began to pour into Paris after World War I, cafés served only coffee, the various *eaux de vie* and the infusions of wines and herbs known as *aperitifs* and *digestifs*. Orders for the

Josephine Baker holding a large feathered cape while looking over her shoulder, smiling and wearing a sparkling costume, 1931

Martini, Old-Fashioned or Cosmopolitan were met with blank stares. The closest to a "mixed drink" was coffee *corrigé*—"corrected"—with a dash of cognac, the *fine à l'eau*—brandy diluted with a little water—and the Toddy or Punch (pronounced *ponch*) that combined *eau de vie* with hot water, sugar and lemon, supposedly as a means of warding off the common cold. This was a favorite drink of Ernest Hemingway. "And we sit outside the Dôme Café," he wrote to Sherwood Anderson, "warmed up against one of those charcoal braziers and it's so damned cold outside and the brazier makes it so warm and we drink rum punch, hot, and the rum enters into us like the Holy Spirit."

Tourism changed everything. "To a certain class of American," wrote Jimmie Charters, barman at the Dingo and the Jockey in Montparnasse, and later at Harry's Bar, across the river, next to the Opera, "drinking in excess became an obligation. No party was a success without complete intoxication of the guests." *Bars Americains* appeared all over Paris, generally manned by African-Americans, often former soldiers who gravitated to France because of its indifference to skin color.

By 1930, *The Savoy Cocktail Book,* an indispensable reference of all barmen, filled 300 pages with recipes for highballs, toddies, fizzes, sours, juleps and coolers. They included the Corpse Reviver (gin, Cointreau and absinthe), Satan's Whiskers (Italian and French vermouth, gin, orange juice and Grand Marnier) and the coffee-colored Josephine Baker (Cognac, apricot brandy, port, lemon zest and an egg yolk.) Gastronomes detested the cocktail society and the crowds of boozy barflies that went with it. Food writer Julian Street, writing in 1929, looked back with nostalgia to the aristocratic debauchery of the *belle époque*, and "nights when a king, a crown prince and a grand duke, each from a different land, competed in buying champagne for the *cocottes* of L'Abbaye until the cold blue light of the Paris dawn came seeping through a skylight."

To composers, jazz and alcohol in general provided the perfect medium for their imagination. Francis Poulenc, Erik Satie and Darius Milhaud created effervescent mixtures of African rhythms and boulevard *chansons* that were, in their way, cocktails of music. Painters struggled to find a similar inspiration. The impetus, when it came, was from popular design.

In 1925, Paul Colin, a young artist from Nancy, received a panic call from a friend at the Théâtre des Champs-Élysées, which was about to present *Revue Nègre* with an imported African-American cast. During rehearsals, the producers had discarded its antiquated plantation and riverboat motifs to showcase the erotic appeal of its chorus line, in particular 19-year-old dancer Josephine Baker. New publicity material was desperately needed.

Colin had his first glimpse of Baker during rehearsal for a last-minute addition to the show, *Danse Sauvage,* a *pas de deux* for which, dressed only in a skirt of feathers, she was carried onstage by a no less naked male dancer. Visiting his studio that night to model for him, Baker woke up in his bed. Exhilarated by his exotic new lover, Colin created posters for the show that projected a wised-up city ambience, with leering black faces and a grinning girl hitching up her skirt to show her legs. He later celebrated his affair with Baker in a portfolio of lithographs, *Le Tumulte noir* (The Black Craze).

Once she joined the Folies Bergère, costumiers and makeup artists converted Baker into a sensuous hybrid of African savagery and trans-Atlantic sass, a cocktail

Paul Colin poster for *Revue Nègre*

condensed into the ballad that became her theme song, *J'ai deux amours: mon pays et Paris* (I Have Two Loves: My Country and Paris.) In a technique that proved effective for Brazilian singer/dancer Carmen Miranda, whom Hollywood dressed in hats topped with a pineapple, Baker was given a skirt of plumply phallic yellow velour bananas.

Inspired by the *Revue Nègre*, American jazz shows poured into Europe. When local musicians protested, the government forced impresarios to employ five French players for every import. Convinced that only black Americans could play jazz, producers continued to hire talent from the U.S., paying their French counterparts to sit backstage. "Jazz" remained a popular label until the 1940s, used to describe anything from clothing and dancing to a style of dress and behavior. In 1946, the magazine *Verve* commissioned a series of cutout collages from Henri Matisse inspired by circus performers and his voyages in the Pacific. Matisse called the collection *Circus,* but the publisher, Tériade, substituted *Jazz,* the label under which it became one of Matisse's best-loved creations.

Nineteen-twenties Montparnasse, bohemian, hard-drinking and liberally furnished with vice, helped create a new market among wealthy foreigners for original art. It revived the career of Kees van Dongen, in the doldrums since the days before World War I when he had been among the leading *Fauves*. Reborn as a society portraitist, he painted film stars Arletty and Maurice Chevalier, as well as such crowned heads as Leopold III of Belgium, and numerous socialites. "The essential thing is to elongate the women and especially to make them slim," he said cynically. "After that it just remains to enlarge their jewels. They are ravished."

The Corn Poppy, Kees van Dongen, c.1919, Museum of Fine Art, Houston

As well as van Dongen, such painters as Chaim Soutine, Moïse Kisling, Tsuguharu Foujita and Julian Pincas, a.k.a. Jules Pascin, were suddenly in demand. The more sensational their work, the better it sold. Soutine achieved notoriety with a series of paintings known as

Le Bœuf écorché (The Flayed Carcass). Hauling a side of beef into his studio, he painted it for weeks, indifferent to the stench. In 1923, American collector Albert C. Barnes, also a patron of Renoir, bought 60 Soutine paintings on the same day. With joyous memories of time spent on the Côte d'Azur during World War I, the artist clattered down the stairs to rue Delambre, hailed a taxi and ordered the driver to take him to Nice, 400 miles away.

CHAPTER 25

MELTED CAMEMBERT AND LIMP FRIED EGGS

Salvador Dalí's The Persistence of Memory

A ttempting to review *The Secret Life of Salvador Dalí,* a fanciful autobiography of the Spanish Surrealist, American humorist James Thurber was forced to concede defeat. "Let me be the first to admit," he wrote, "that the naked truth about me is to the naked truth about Salvador Dalí as an old ukulele in the attic is to a piano in a tree, and I mean a piano *with breasts.*"

Dalí and Gala at the dinner and costume ball at the Del Monte Hotel in Pebble Beach in 1941

Never one to skimp on exaggeration, Dalí claimed mastery not only of the studio and bedroom but of the kitchen as well. He claimed to have begun cooking at the age of 6, though it's debatable whether or not his recipes were edible. In cooking meat, he advised retaining the bones, and, in the case of lobster, shrimp or snails, the shells also. "The most philosophical organs man possesses," he wrote, "are his jaws. It is at the supreme moment of reaching the marrow of anything that you discover the very taste of truth."

Food lies at the heart of many Dalí paintings. He first sensed intimations of its future importance in 1931, at the conclusion of a Parisian dinner party. Too tired to accompany his wife, Gala, and her friends to a late-night cabaret, he remained at the table, surrounded by the debris of supper. His thoughts returned to the half-completed canvas in his studio. He'd hoped to reflect on the imprecision of memory and our tendency to distort, if not delete entirely, that which we find unpalatable, but for the moment he'd reached an impasse.

He had already painted the background, a neutral landscape, flat as a table, interrupted only by a distant headland and some enigmatic slabs, one of them topped by the gaunt branches of a dead tree. In the foreground lay a mysterious figure, its only recognizably human feature a single large eye, closed in sleep.

Some element was needed to bind all these elements into a coherent whole; a metaphor to suggest our shifting, elastic, melting perception of reality. At that moment, Dalí's eyes fell on a half-eaten Camembert cheese among the remains of the meal. Deliquescent at

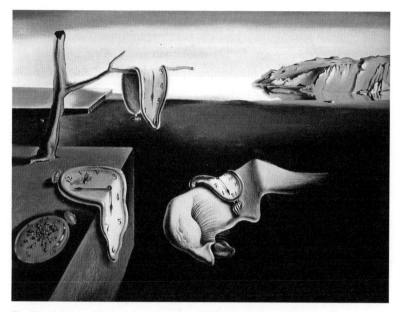

The Persistence of Memory, Salvador Dalí, 1931, Museum of Modern Art

room temperature, the interior had oozed out onto the wooden table, the surface of the drying cheese as glossy as porcelain.

Seized with inspiration, Dalí hurried to his studio. Snatching up his palette, he smeared together white and yellow pigments and began furiously to paint. By the time Gala returned, he had enhanced the landscape with three clock faces, draped, limp as fried eggs, over a branch of his dead tree, the edge of one featureless slab, and, saddle-like, over the sleeping foreground figure. Large as plates and droopy as gloves, these "soft watches" would appear in his work for the next 30 years, a metaphor as distinctive as it was enigmatic.

With this painting, *The Persistence of Memory*, Dalí had arrived, and his emblem under which he would conquer the art world was food. Alert now to the power of culinary metaphors, he added eggs to his artistic larder. In every size from the minuscule to the gargantuan, sometimes fried, more often raw, they populate his work. One scholarly analysis suggests they represent "the Christian symbol of the resurrection of Christ, but also act as an emblem of purity and perfection, as well as evoking concepts of uterine memory and rebirth"—not inappropriate for an artist who insisted he could remember every detail of his life, right back to the womb.

Dalí had a special affection for the *oursin* or sea urchin. Not only did the brittle shell and ovoid shape resemble those of an egg; its pink, slightly scented roe was itself made up of countless tiny eggs. As early as 1929, his film *Un chien andalou,* made in collaboration with Luis Buñuel, dissolves from a woman's hairy armpit to a sea urchin's black-spined shell. True to this sexual subtext, Dalí, rather than eating the *oursin* in the customary manner, scraping the raw roe from its shell, preferred it mixed with chocolate, supposedly a traditional Catalan aphrodisiac.

During his first days as a member of the Surrealists, experimenting with juxtaposing unrelated objects to create a fresh and unexpected reality, Dalí filled the pockets of a dinner jacket with small glasses of milk, an object he called *Le Veston aphrodisiaque* (The Aphrodisiac Dinner Jacket). Previewing the work to the assembled brotherhood at one of its nightly *séances*, he was attacked by André Breton's lieutenant Louis Aragon, then a strict Stalinist, on the grounds that it wasted milk while women and children in Paris were starving. When the piece went on show in a gallery, Dalí replaced the milk with *crème de menthe,* only to find that his helper, directed to keep the glasses filled as the liqueur evaporated, was actually drinking it. This practice halted abruptly when Dalí replaced *crème de menthe* with green ink.

The love of Dalí's life was his partner and eventual wife, Gala. Formerly married to Surrealist poet Paul Éluard, she was 10 years older than Dalí, and much more sexually sophisticated, having shared a *ménage à trois* with Éluard and painter Max Ernst. Primarily a voyeur, Dalí derived most satisfaction from watching the sexual activities of others, including Gala. He took a similarly detached view of food, preferring to write about and paint it rather than eat it. These preoccupations converged when he used Gala as a model. At various times, he painted her with a loaf of bread balanced on her head, and with two lamb chops on her shoulder.

In 1937, asked to propose film ideas for the Marx Brothers, Dalí had suggested a banquet at which guests sat not at a long table but occupied an enormous bed. In September 1941, stranded in California by the war, he drew on the same idea for a dinner and costume ball at the Del Monte Hotel in Pebble Beach. The theme was *Night in a Surrealist Forest,* and guests were asked to dress so as to recall their worst nightmare. Supposedly a fund-raiser for artists in exile, the event attracted such celebrities as Bob Hope, Bing Crosby, Jack Benny and Ginger Rogers. As Gala, her costume topped by a

Les Dîners de Gala

unicorn headdress, reclined on a red velvet bed, guests
were served the fish course in a high-heeled shoe. Lifting
the metal cover of the second course, they found live
frogs.

In 1973, a lavish cookbook, *Les Dîners de Gala,*
appeared under Dalí's name. "Don't look for dietetic
formulas here," warned the introduction. "If you are a
disciple of one of those calorie-counters who turn the
joys of eating into a form of punishment, close this
book at once; it is too lively, too aggressive, and far too
impertinent for you." Recipes, each illustrated with a
Dalí painting, were arranged under such headings as
"Sodomized Entrées." They included Thousand Year
Old Eggs, Roast Peacock, Frog Pasties, and Veal Cutlets
stuffed with Snails. The chapter devoted to aphrodisiacs
included recipes for a Casanova Cocktail and Stewed Beef
Eros.

Les Dîners de Gala was the brainchild of Dalí's secretary and business manager, Captain Peter Moore. Aside from the illustrations, the artist had little to do with it, nor were its recipes intended to be practical. Despite claims of precocious culinary talent, Dalí was no cook, preferring to dine on room service delivered to his suite at Paris's luxurious Hotel Meurice. Favorite venues in New York included the Russian Tea Room, one of whose waiters he recruited to model for his painting *Christopher Columbus*, and the King Cole Lounge of the St. Regis Hotel, where the anal Dalí particularly enjoyed its Maxfield Parrish mural showing the reaction among King Cole's courtiers as his majesty expels a fart. When he did visit a restaurant, invariably without making a reservation, he took the best table, ordered a lavish meal for his retinue, then departed with a lordly order to send the bill to his hotel, where it was ignored.

CHAPTER 26

THE FOOD FRONT

Surviving the German Occupation by rationing, foraging and "Party Surprise"

O nce France capitulated to the Germans in 1940, the invaders lost no time in imposing their Teutonic will. Determined to humiliate the victors of World War I, Hitler forced France's high command to sign the instrument of surrender in the same railway car in which Germany admitted defeat in 1918. In addition, France was forced to bear the costs of its own occupation.

Paris and the coasts remained under direct military control. The rest of France was administered from the

German soldiers at Restaurant à La Mère Catherine, in Place du Tertre, Montmartre, June 1940

spa town of Vichy by a puppet government under World War I hero Marshal Philippe Pétain. In Paris, German generals seized the best hotels and mansions and systematically set about looting the country, shipping back to Berlin everything from the treasures of its museums to 60 percent of its agricultural produce. Called up for their obligatory two years of military service, young men were shipped to Germany and forced to work in factories. Germany's air force, the Luftwaffe, took over the Palais de Luxembourg and, as food became scarce, dug up its famous formal gardens, laid out in 1612 by Marie de Médicis, to plant potatoes and cabbages.

Parisians did their best to live as if the Occupation was not taking place. Without gas to run their cars, cabdrivers fitted bicycles with an enclosed cabin large enough for a single passenger. A curfew forced everyone indoors by 10 p.m. After that, streetlights operating on diminished power kept the City of Light in perpetual gloom.

Like many Parisiennes, future screen star Leslie Caron, then a child, experienced the Occupation mainly in terms of food, or its absence. Moving to the country, her family lived mostly on what they could forage. "My mother tried to feed us with seaweed she picked on the beach and dandelions from the railroad tracks," Caron recalled. "The seaweed was inedible—a disaster." Fortunately their housekeeper came from Burgundy and knew how to collect snails and edible plants, and to spin out the little meat available. Even so, Caron's health, like that of most children, suffered from this deprivation. She was given horse blood to build up her strength, and her father, a pharmacist, stole some of the cocoa butter supplied to grease anal suppositories, a popular remedy in the French pharmacopeia. Caron got used to every fried dish having the flavor of chocolate.

None of these restrictions applied to the Germans or to their collaborators. What they couldn't divert from export was acquired through a thriving black market. Among the best films to come out of the war, Claude Autant-Lara's 1946 comedy *La Traversée de Paris* (Four Bags Full) featured Bourvil and Jean Gabin manhandling four suitcases of pork across the blacked-out city. Bertrand Tavernier's 2002 film, *Laissez-Passer* (Safe Conduct), dealt with the Occupation's effect on the crippled French film industry. A period film has to be suspended because the extras eat all the food from the table in a banquet scene. Ernst Lubitsch caught the prevailing nostalgia for food in his film *To Be or Not to Be*. While being entertained by the head of the Gestapo, intent on seduction, actress Carole Lombard, used to the high life, almost faints when she sees the supper he's prepared. "Champagne and caviar," she sighs. "Then they still exist!"

In real life, the French did their best simply to survive. "Life is hard," wrote one Parisian in 1944. "Everyone grows thinner. A kilo of butter costs 1,000 francs. A kilo of peas 45 francs. A kilo of potatoes 40 francs. Still we must find them." Hunger didn't suppress the French instinct towards coquetry; may even, in fact, have stimulated it. Even pro-Nazi magazines carried fashion tips—with stockings a thing of the past, women drew a line with eyebrow pencil down the back of each leg in imitation of a seam. Soldiers risked death to salvage the small silk parachutes attached to flares, which their womenfolk turned into lingerie.

Partie Surprise, André Pécoud

Among those who remained in the city, the vogue was for the so-called *partie surprise.* Unlike the Anglo-Saxon event for which it was named, the French *partie surprise* was no surprise. Friends converged on the home of the host, each bringing whatever ingredient they had managed to acquire. Turning such miscellaneous constituents into a meal challenged even the most inventive chef, inspiring such dishes as North Sea Bouillabaisse, a variation on the Mediterranean fish stew that replaced onion and garlic with potatoes and turnips, and *rascasse* and *loup de mer* with cod and dogfish.

Under *Systéme D* (for *débrouiller,* i.e, to manage or get by), the Ministry of Food introduced rationing to make the most efficient use of what was available. Meat was mainly mince, of dubious provenance. Leslie Caron recalled:

> *I remember endless hachis parmentier, Shepherd's Pie, or hash and mash. For vegetables, we were down to animal fodder: salsify, rutabagas, Jerusalem artichokes, all three previously unknown to Parisians. Fruit was as rare and expensive as tobacco. Children had one glass of milk a day. We were each given an ever-shrinking ration of butter; it eventually amounted to an eggcup full per person, per week. By the end of the war, bread was down to one slice a day per person: two-thirds flour, one-third sawdust.*

As wheat disappeared, bakers substituted the animal feed alfalfa. Coffee was approximated by the herb chicory, mixed with roasted barley or acorns, sugar extracted from licorice and even pumpkins, while cigarettes were filled with a mixture of dried grass and herbs optimistically called "National Tobacco."

Threatened as Jews with internment or even worse, Gertrude Stein and her companion Alice B. Toklas appealed to Americophile Bernard Fay, an old friend but also a prominent collaborator and associate of Marshal Pétain, who appointed him director of the Bibliothèque Nationale. Fay agreed to protect Stein's art collection from seizure by the Nazis. He also had the couple moved to safety in Bilignin, a village deep in Vichy territory, where they lived out the war in well-fed comfort. Jailed in 1946, Fay escaped to Switzerland in 1951 thanks to money supplied by Toklas.

CHAPTER 27

THE CHICKEN FROM HELL

New French favorites from India, Russia, China and Vietnam

I n 1978, actor Peter Ustinov was working in Kenya on the film *Ashanti*. Bored with the unit caterer's food, he and some friends, hoping to find a restaurant, set out to cross the border into Tanzania.

The frontier police had other ideas, particularly since none of the film people had visas.

Claudette Colbert with John Barrymore in a scene from the film, *Midnight*, 1939

"But we're not staying," Ustinov pleaded. "Just long enough to eat at a restaurant."

The guard jumped on this. "*Which* restaurant?"

Ustinov had a brainwave. "The Chinese restaurant, of course."

Satisfied, the guard lifted the barrier and waved them through.

Ustinov's guess was inspired. If a town anywhere in the world has an ethnic restaurant, it is almost certainly Chinese.

The explosion of Asian food across the Anglo-Saxon world was a phenomenon of the early 20th century. One of the first Chinese restaurants in Europe opened in London's West End just after World War I. Its proprietor, Bool-yun "Brilliant" Chang, used it as a front for smuggling drugs into Britain. By the late-1920s, Asian food was still sufficiently rare to attract the following summary in a 1927 guidebook for American visitors to Paris:

CHINESE RESTAURANT.
Rue de Carmes. Off rue des Ecoles. See dozens of Chinese men with white girls. A Chinese dinner. A clean place, interestingly decorated. A great novelty.

The Chinese were pioneers in adapting their traditional cuisine to Western tastes, followed by Indian restaurants or, more often, Pakistani and Sri Lankan. Within a few years, most of the Western world was eating Vietnamese *nems* (spring rolls), Japanese sushi and Korean grilled beef with kim chi (pickled cabbage with chili). Benelong in Paris served a grilled fillet of

kangaroo, and in Los Angeles, Wallaby Darned offered
authentic Down Under meat pies.

The incursion of Mexican food into North
America has the logic of geography. Harder to explain
is the popularity in Britain of Indian food, an invasion
so complete that the nation's favorite meal is no longer
fish and chips or roast beef with Yorkshire pudding but
chicken tikka masala, an Indian dish of chicken in a
creamy tomato and yogurt sauce. Even more puzzlingly,
France's traditional *steak frites* (steak and french fries)
is now under threat from the *couscous* of North
Africa, Belgian stewed mussels and even the American
hamburger.

London could also boast the West's first Indian
restaurant. Veeraswamy opened in 1926, just off Regent
Street, next to the theater district of Shaftesbury Avenue.
Many retired English military men and civil servants
were nostalgic for the curries of India. The presence of
a doorman in traditional Indian dress reassured them
they would be served only authentic dishes, correctly
spiced, but not every restaurant was so conscientious.
As Indian cooks moderated the use of chili, Chinese
chefs altered traditional dishes to accommodate Western
taste, and avoided contentious ingredients. In Dublin, a
health inspector closed a Chinese restaurant after finding
the remains of a German Shepherd in its kitchen. It
reopened when the owner testified that this delicacy was
never wasted on Irish clients but reserved for family and
friends.

Certain Asian dishes achieved instant popularity.
They included *tandoori*, for which pieces of meat
marinated in yogurt and spices were cooked in a

clay oven or *tandoor*, and Chinese *dim sum*. As these dumplings, steamed and served in bamboo baskets, became a popular choice for lunch, restaurateurs omitted to mention that, in China, they were generally eaten at breakfast.

The ability to ingest highly spiced food became a test of masculinity. Attending a literary festival in Wales, Australian poet Les Murray was taken by some local writers to an Indian restaurant. Ignoring "the kindly brown waiter wringing the hands of dissuasion," he ordered the most incendiary dish on the menu, chicken vindaloo. Spiced with cumin, mustard seed, cinnamon, cloves, turmeric, paprika and, naturally, cayenne pepper, this is not for amateurs, but Murray, ignoring the waiter's advice—"Oh, vindaloo, sir! You sure you want vindaloo, sir?"—trusted a palate seasoned, so he thought, by long experience. His poem *Vindaloo in Merthyr Tydfil* documented its effects:

> *Fair play, it was frightful. I spooned the chicken of Hell*
> *In a sauce of rich yellow brimstone. The valley boys with me,*
> *Tasting it, croaked to white Jesus.*

Following the 1917 Russian Revolution, 200,000 refugees poured into France, some with their fortunes intact, others penniless. Impoverished grand duchesses became *vendeuses* or governesses while one-time counts took jobs as doormen or cabdrivers: By 1939, Paris's Union of Russian Cabdrivers had 3,000 members.

Wealthier émigrés funded orphanages for Russian children, homes for the aged and an Orthodox cathedral. Publishers issued Russian-language books and newspapers.

At the Albatros studios in suburban Montreuil-sur-Bois, Alexander Kamenka produced films with Russian actors and technicians. Scores of restaurants opened across France to accommodate those who could still afford caviar, champagne and a *shashlik* of lamb doused in brandy and carried to the table impaled on a sword, and in flames. Those without money kept to the shadows, nursing a vodka and weeping as the balalaikas throbbed and another exile sang of the nation and the friends they would never see again.

Stories of Paris's Russian community provided Hollywood with plenty of new stories, the cinema reflecting a society not unlike that of Hollywood itself, where one could adopt any persona that one could make convincing. In one notable misstep, Metro-Goldwyn-Mayer, richest of the studios, produced *Rasputin and the Empress*, a fanciful reconstruction of the fall of the Romanovs and the baleful influence of the monk Grigori Rasputin on the susceptible czarina and her ladies-in-waiting, one of whom, based on Princess Irina Romanova Youssoupoff, he rapes. Her lawsuit alleging invasion of privacy and libel yielded a judgment of $127,373 in the English courts and an out-of-court settlement in New York, reportedly for $1 million. Thereafter, every Hollywood film bore the disclaimer, "This motion picture is a work of fiction and any resemblance to persons living or dead is purely coincidental."

Other films inspired by the Russian exiles were no less melodramatic. In Josef von Sternberg's *The Last Command*, Emil Jannings plays a former general, now working as a movie extra, who finds himself acting in a film of his greatest military triumph, directed by the former Bolshevik whom, while a general, he sentenced to death by firing squad. In *Midnight,* written by Billy Wilder, penniless chorus girl Claudette Colbert, dumped in a rain-swept Paris with nothing in her purse but a pawn ticket for her luggage, wakes up in a suite at the Ritz, registered as a Hungarian aristocrat, the Countess Czerny. Both Anatole Litvak's *Tovarich* and Ernst Lubitsch's *Ninotchka*, also part-written by Wilder (and both set in Paris), wrung a bitter laugh from the émigrés' plight. In *Tovarich,* adapted from Jacques Deval's play, Charles Boyer and Claudette Colbert, entrusted with the Russian crown jewels, live in poverty in Paris rather than betray that trust. Taking jobs as butler and lady's maid, they charm and educate their bourgeois employers.

Food, a secondary motif in *Midnight*—to demonstrate the eccentricity of her supposed husband's family, Colbert confides, "His grandfather sent me, as an engagement present, one roller skate, covered with Thousand Island dressing"—emerges full-blown in *Ninotchka* to highlight the cultural differences between Greta Garbo's humorless commissar and the suave playboy who seduces her. When, in a Paris restaurant, Garbo orders raw beets and carrots, the proprietor, offended, says, "Madame, this is a restaurant, not a meadow," while at the conclusion, three Russian bureaucrats, Buljanoff, Iranoff and Kopalski, weaponize food by opening a restaurant.

> *NINOTCHKA. You mean you are deserting Russia?*
> *KOPALSKI. Don't call it desertion. Our*
> *little restaurant ... that is our Russia ... the Russia*

Greta Garbo with Sig Ruman, Alexander Granach, and Felix Bressart in *Ninotchka*, 1939

of borscht, the Russia of beef Stroganoff, blinis with
sour cream ...
IRANOFF ... the Russia of piroshki ... people will eat
and love it.

Just as none of the actors playing Buljanoff, Iranoff and Kopalski was actually born in Russia, the restaurant they open is not in Paris but Istanbul. Having lived in France, Billy Wilder would have known that, of all European nations, it is the least welcoming to foreign food. A restaurant may advertise Chinese or Japanese or Indian cuisine, but the food it serves will have been altered out of all recognition to suit French tastes. The French version of chili is indistinguishable from baked beans. And a French curry? Over some things, it is more diplomatic to draw a veil.

Even McDonalds failed in its first attempt to introduce hamburgers to the French. The second, instigated by a Frenchman, varied the burger recipe to take account of local tastes. More importantly, it opened its restaurants not in working-class areas but on such fashionable thoroughfares as the Champs-Élysées. Once the *jeunesse dorée* embraced the Big Mac, success was assured.

Furious, McDonalds' U.S. management employed every dirty trick to shut down the French franchisee. They succeeded on a technicality. The beef in the French patty contained less fat, the frites were thinner and crisper, and beer joined shakes on the menu— offenses against a contract that required the McDonalds experience to be identical no matter where it was bought. A few years later, McDonalds started up again in France with great success: with less fat in the meat and beer on sale (as in the Netherlands, Austria and Germany as well).

CHAPTER 28

STARS
OF THE STOVE

*Carême and Escoffier to Soyer
and Child*

S ean Kinsella, chef and owner during the 1970s
and '80s of Dublin's most distinguished restaurant,
the Mirabeau, made only minimal concessions
to the eating public. His establishment on a quiet
side street in Sandycove barely advertised its existence.
Instead, one looked for his Rolls-Royce parked outside.
The menu had no prices. If you had to ask, you couldn't
afford them.

Le Chef de l'Hôtel Chatham, William Orpen, 1921, Royal Academy of Arts, London

Waiting for their table, patrons relaxed in a lounge over a glass of wine. Periodically, waiters circled the room with salvers on which rested a leg of lamb, a fillet of venison, a whole salmon.

"The *côte de boeuf*," they murmured, pausing before each party. "The trout."

One well-lubricated client couldn't resist a joke. As the next waiter departed, he said loudly after him, "If none of you want it, I'll have it."

Nobody laughed. Facetiousness was as misplaced here as in St. Patrick's Cathedral.

Dinner passed well enough until the bill arrived. After a quick addition, the jokester called back the waiter.

"Look here, pal," he said. "Your sums don't add up. You've overcharged me a fiver."

With a startled look, the man disappeared, but returned shortly after, followed by Kinsella himself, still wearing his chef's *tablier* and *toque*.

Snatching the bill, he did a quick calculation.

"You are correct, sir," he said. "Our calculations were in error."

Crumpling the bill with one hand, he dropped it to the floor. "... and accordingly there will be no charge for your meal tonight ..."

Before the man could stammer his thanks, Kinsella leaned forward until his face was only a few centimeters from that of the customer.

"... but," he growled, "I never want to see you in my restaurant again."

Although the celebrity chef and his accompanying myths often appear a 21st-century creation, born of the

Marie-Antoine Carême

shotgun marriage between reality TV and the restaurant culture, their roots lie more than two centuries back, at the moment when revolution, in destroying France's great houses, threw their most gifted servants onto the open market. Some remained in France and opened restaurants. Others went to the few surviving great houses, often outside France. Carême cooked for Britain's Prince Regent at the Brighton Pavilion and for Czar Alexander I of Russia at the Winter Palace. Georges-Auguste Escoffier, in partnership with César Ritz, managed London's Savoy Hotel and, later, Paris's Ritz.

These culinary hired guns were the first food professionals to recognize that image counted as much as expertise. Even more than today's Gordon Ramsay, Jamie Oliver and Wolfgang Puck, they were showmen, ready to demonstrate their expertise for all who could meet their price. For Nellie Melba, Escoffier created Melba

Alexis Soyer demonstrates his stove during the Crimean War

Toast and Pêche Melba. He also arranged a banquet in which the initial letters of the dishes spelled out the hostess's name, and another for a gambling syndicate that won a fortune betting Red Nine. All the food was red and the number nine dominated the menu. Anyone arranging a dinner did so in collaboration with the *chef de cuisine*, who advised not only on which ingredients were at their best, but ensured that sworn enemies were not seated next to one another, nor mistresses next to wives.

No 19th-century chef was more flamboyant than Alexis Soyer. Fleeing an increasingly unstable continental Europe, he took over the kitchens of London's Reform Club in 1837, installing gas ovens and refrigeration. While Carême shared the sartorial sense of his masters and personally designed the white cotton *toque* and apron now the chef's standard uniform, Soyer's clothes reflected his eccentricity. According to one description:

> *He wore a kind of paletôt* [double breasted jacket] *of light camlet cloth, with voluminous lapels and deep cuffs of lavender watered silk; very baggy trousers, with lavender stripes down the seams; very shiny boots and quite as glossy a hat; his attire being completed by tightly-fitting gloves, of the hue known in Paris as beurre frais* (fresh butter)—*that is to say, light yellow. Every article of his attire was cut on what dressmakers call a "bias," or as he used to designate it 'à la zoug-zoug'* [zig-zag]. *He* [had] *an unconquerable aversion from any garment which exhibited either horizontal or perpendicular lines. His very visiting-cards, his cigar-case, and the handle of his cane took slightly oblique inclinations.*

Exceptionally for the self-interested culture of the kitchen, Soyer had an active social conscience. Having visited the Crimea and seen troops cooking their meals over tiny open fires, always at risk from snipers, he designed a field stove that burned almost any fuel but never showed a light. It was still in use in the 1980s. He also reorganized the provisioning of army hospitals, and trained and installed in every regiment a "Regimental

Georges-Auguste Escoffier

cook," eventually to evolve into the Army Catering Corps.

Less successfully, he also intervened to alleviate the 1847 famine in Ireland following the failure of the potato crop. As well as contributing money from the income from his books, he created an economical Famine Soup that used a minimum of meat, eked out with the leaves and trimmings of vegetables that most chefs consigned to the garbage. Stung by critics who charged that a *bouillon* of 12 pounds of beef to 100 gallons of water was barely soup at all, Soyer traveled to Dublin and set up a soup kitchen that fed tens of thousands who would otherwise have starved. William Makepeace Thackeray's 1849 novel *The History of Pendennis* included a character named "Alcide Mirobolant," widely recognised as a parody of Soyer. ("*Mirobolant*" is French for "fabulous" or "astonishing.")

Soyer's philanthropy contrasts with the underhanded behavior of the dignified and superficially respectable Escoffier. While managing the Savoy, he and Ritz skimmed a fortune in kickbacks from food and wine suppliers. Waiters were urged to push champagne, since wine merchants paid a bonus on every cork returned. Escoffier even set up a fake company to sell food to the hotel at inflated prices and an agency for kitchen staff that charged the Savoy for hiring his own appointees. On March 8, 1898, Escoffier, Ritz and their entire kitchen staff were dismissed for "gross negligence and breaches of duty and mismanagement." A newspaper reported, "Sixteen fiery French and Swiss cooks (some of them took their long knives and placed themselves in a position of defiance) have been bundled out by the aid of a strong force of Metropolitan police." With Escoffier, Ritz moved to Paris and took over the hotel bearing his name, the cellars and kitchens of which were already filled with supplies paid for by the Savoy.

Had television existed in Victorian times, Soyer's instant stardom would have been assured. Pioneered by Julia Child, the cookery show proved the most durable and economical of all programs, requiring only a simple set and a performer with the personality, as dictated by the first rule of marketing, to "sell the sizzle, not the steak." Few viewers ever tried the dishes demonstrated. As in pornography, watching the process was enough.

Young Cook in the Kitchen, Joseph Bail, 1893

The "secret sauce" of the cookery show was alcohol. Ever since *The Galloping Gourmet*, Graham Kerr, pioneered the practice of cooking with a glass of wine in hand and insisted that most dishes benefited from "a short slope of sherry," alcohol was a constant of TV cookery, contributing to the flair that characterized the best performers. The 1950s demonstrations by British chef Fanny Cradock were sufficiently popular to fill the 5,000 seats of London's Royal Albert Hall, notwithstanding husband Johnny's obvious inebriation. A bottle or two of wine also accounted for the on-air ebullience of *Floyd on Food's* Keith Floyd, as well as his convictions for driving under the influence.

Among the canvases of those 19th-century painters who took cooks as their subjects, alcohol is also omnipresent. The numerous images of young cooks by Joseph Bail and Théodule Ribot, working in the documentary style of Chardin, include one of a pot boy sneaking a bottle of wine. William Orpen's 1921 *Le Chef de l'Hôtel Chatham*, proud of the beard he's permitted to grow as a badge of his importance, stands with hands on hips, *toque* and *tablier* worn with all the confidence of a military officer—and, inevitably, a bottle of wine and half-filled glass at his elbow.

CHAPTER 29

FOOD HEAVEN

The culinary traditions of France

W hy do people come to France from all over the world to eat? One of the more imaginative theories was proposed by American science fiction writer William Gibson. As our bodies are whisked at supersonic speeds from continent to continent, our souls, and thus our five senses, struggle to keep up. If the journey is long—say Los Angeles to Paris—they don't arrive at the same time. Sight and taste set down first; touch, hearing and smell rejoin our bodies only after.

Why else do new arrivals, waking on their first morning in Paris, stare out at the skyline in mute appreciation, spend a morning strolling around the

Salon du Chocolat 2013–Fashion Chocolate Show at Porte de Versailles

The dish by chef Alan Ducasse on the table in the dining room

city in silent awe, then enter, famished, a promising restaurant?

The French waiter learns early to accommodate them. Nodding amiably at their struggling Franglais, he delivers their order to the kitchen, then returns with slices of fresh baguette, the golden crust crisp but yielding, the interior white and elastic. He may also include a few pats of butter, their dairy richness set off with crystals of sea salt that crunch deliciously between the teeth.

And then wine. Of course, there must be wine. A meal without wine is like a kiss without a cuddle, a boiled egg without salt. The carafe of cabernet franc from the Languedoc does more than satisfy the thirst. It nourishes the very soul.

With their two resident senses now fully engaged, the visitors turn their eyes to the door to the kitchen, from which, in a few seconds, will issue wonders . . .

Well, perhaps it isn't always like that. Rubbery veal, overcooked *confit de canard,* and suspiciously fishy *cabillaud* appear in even the best restaurants. The cheapness of precooked dishes can corrupt even the most resolute graduate of the *Cordon Bleu.*

In many countries, there's nothing else. Even in France, as farmers' markets wither away, their place is taken by professional-only supermarkets selling vacuum-packed and frozen Chateaubriand and 50-gallon cans of precooked *frites.* Fortunately, the French government regards acquiring and preparing food as part of the *patrimoine*—the national heritage. An infrastructure exists to protect the supply of fresh produce and the means of conveying it to the table at maximum freshness.

To support this effort, regional authorities hold annual food fairs celebrating local cheese, wine, fruit, seafood and meat: *cassoulet* in Toulouse, truffles in Périgord, tiny Mirabelle plums in Nancy, chocolate at the Salon du Chocolat in Paris and wine everywhere.

Visit a street market anywhere in Paris, and you will find one or two professionals joining the housewives in sniffing, weighing and assessing each item, then filling their baskets with lettuce of maximum crispness and peaches at the peak of their perfume and juiciness.

At such places, one sees the French culinary tradition at its richest. A *fromager* carves a slice of elephant-skinned Saint-Nectaire from a giant wheel and offers it on his knife, while the *boucher* is more than happy to debone and roll a *gigot* of lamb to be roasted for Sunday lunch, or explain the differences between a yellow chicken from Loué and a black-legged bird from Houdan.

Even the professional restaurateur can be overwhelmed by the cornucopia of French produce. Opening his first restaurant in Paris, Australian chef Jean-Paul Bruneteau could barely contain his exhilaration. "I've never had such sweet strawberries, juicy pineapples, ripe bananas, ripe tomatoes," he said. "No hydroponic lettuce. Six kinds of butters to choose from. No margarine in sight. It's food heaven here, really. Gorgeous, gorgeous, *gorgeous* food!"

In such a culture, it's hardly surprising that food and its preparation should remain, as it has for centuries, a continuing preoccupation of French artists. In the cinema and TV alone, as well as the ubiquitous TV cooking programs, a filmmaker has celebrated the first woman to become head chef at the Élysée palace, showing her preparing truffle sandwiches for a dying president. Another confected a feel-good fantasy about the possibility, however remote, of a refugee family of cooks from India relocating in a French village and successfully collaborating with a traditional Michelin-starred restaurant. None, however, could quite compete with the Pixar studio's *Ratatouille,* the animated film about the instincts of a great chef appearing miraculously in the spirit of a Parisian rat. Now that Hollywood, has embraced this most precious of France's cultural treasures, its continuing survival seems assured.

A GASTRONOMICAL PARIS

In an era when the speed at which food is served counts for more than its quality; when restaurants crank up the ambient sound as an encouragement for diners to eat faster; when almost everything served by even the most prestigious establishments has been cooked elsewhere and arrives in the kitchen frozen and freeze-dried, the days when food signified more than sustenance seem impossibly distant.

At such times, I take consolation from Jean Renoir's 1939 film *La Règle du jeu* (The Rules of the Game). Set in the years before World War II, it can seem the record of an even more distant past. The *nouveau riche* Marquis de la Chesnaye hosts a hunting party at his chateau, to the frustration of his chef, who must accommodate the foibles of the guests. When one demands her food contain only sea salt, he blows up. "Diets I accept," he says, "but fads? Forget it!"

Many of Chesnaye's supposed friends are contemptuous of his Jewishness, his rich German wife, his childlike delight in his collection of automatons, but his chef is more respectful.

As he explains, the classic recipe for potato salad requires that the potatoes be peeled while still hot, then doused with white wine. When a lazy *sous-chef* allowed the potatoes to cool before peeling them, the marquis detected the difference, and complained.

"Say what you like," says the chef, "but someone who would notice that is *a man of quality.*"

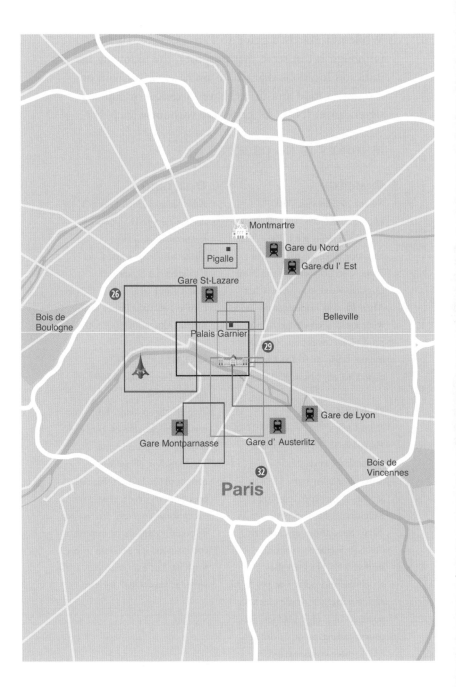

Montmartre

Gare du Nord

Gare du l' Est

Pigalle

Gare St-Lazare

26

Bois de
Boulogne

Palais Garnier

Belleville

29

Gare de Lyon

Gare Montparnasse

Gare d' Austerlitz

Bois de
Vincennes

32

Paris

While not exactly a guide to Paris's best restaurants (although it can serve that purpose), the following list indicates locations that, to an overseas visitor with an interest in food and drink, have historical or culinary significance. (N.B. All prices are without wine.)

IF MONEY IS NO OBJECT . . .

❶ ARPÈGE

84 rue de Varenne, 75007
alain-passard.com
Three Michelin stars. By common consent the best in Paris. Certainly one of the most original—and expensive. Chef Alain Passard no longer cooks with meat, a challenge to his prodigious invention. Tasting menus begin at €145. Evenings, expect to pay about €500 each.

❷ L'EPICURE

Bristol Hotel, 112 rue du Faubourg St.-Honoré, 75008
lebristolparis.com
Three Michelin stars. Chosen as one of the Top Ten Paris Restaurants by TripAdvisor 2016. Specialities of chef Éric Fréchon include macaroni stuffed with black truffles, artichoke and duck *foie gras*, and, bizarrely, a whole chicken poached in a pig's bladder. Six-course tasting menu at dinner €320, three courses €145.

❸ LE CINQ

Four Seasons Hotel George V. 31 avenue George V, 75008
restaurant-lecinq.com
Three Michelin stars. Chef Christian Le Squer offers lunch (four courses) €145, (six courses) €210. Dinner tasting menu (nine courses) €310.

❹ TAILLEVENT

15 rue Lamennais, 75008
taillevent.com
Two Michelin stars. Taillevent was the nickname of 14th-century chef Guillaume Tirel, author of the first cookbook in French. Austere postmodern decor, classic menu, exceptional courtesy. Perfect for a special event, or to impress a companion. It's possible to eat for €50, but expect to pay, with wine, at least €400 for two.

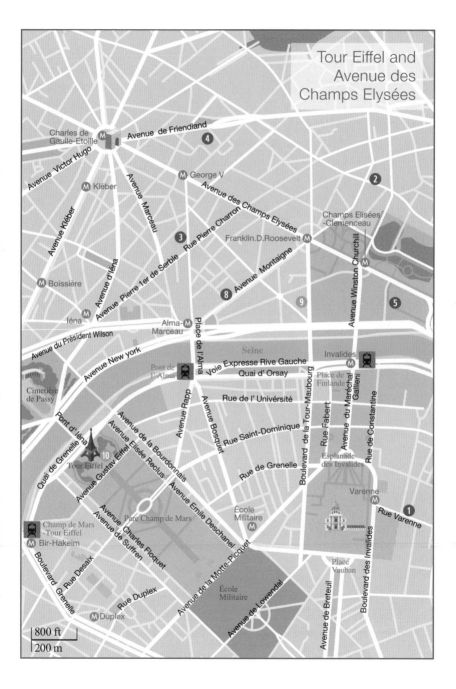

Tour Eiffel and
Avenue des
Champs Elysées

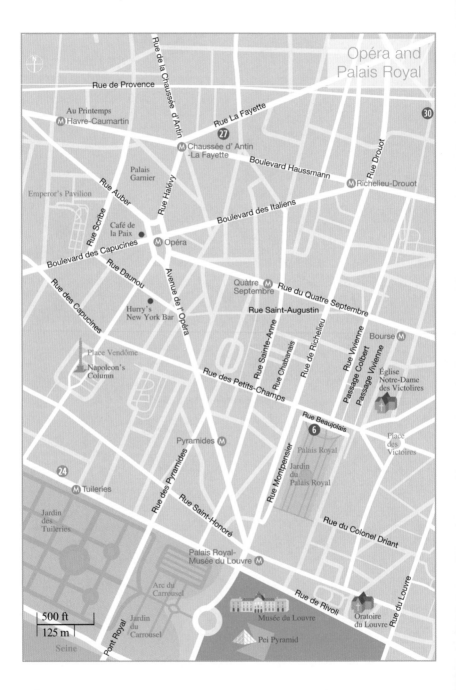

Opéra and
Palais Royal

Rue de Provence

Au Printemps
Ⓜ Havre-Caumartin

Rue de la Chaussée d'Antin

Rue La Fayette

㉗ Chaussée d' Antin
-La Fayette

Boulevard Haussmann

Rue Drouot

㉚

Palais
Garnier

Rue Auber

Rue Halévy

Ⓜ Richelieu-Drouot

Emperor's Pavilion

Rue Scribe

Boulevard des Italiens

Café de
la Paix ●

Boulevard des Capucines

Ⓜ Opéra

Rue Daunou

Avenue de l'Opéra

Rue des Capucines

Quàtre
Septembre

Ⓜ Rue du Quatre Septembre

Rue Saint-Augustin

Hurry's
New York Bar

Rue Sainte-Anne

Rue Chabanais

Rue de Richelieu

Rue Vivienne

Bourse Ⓜ

Passage Colbert

Passage Vivienne

Place Vendôme

Napoleon's
Column

Rue des Petits-Champs

Église
Notre-Dame
des Victoires

Rue Beaujolais

❻

Pyramides Ⓜ

Rue Montpensier

Palais Royal

Place
des
Victoires

㉔

Jardin
du
Palais Royal

Ⓜ Tuileries

Rue des Pyramides

Rue Saint-Honoré

Rue du Colonel Driant

Jardin
des
Tuileries

Palais Royal-
Musée du Louvre Ⓜ

Arc du
Carrousel

Rue de Rivoli

Rue du Louvre

500 ft

Pont Royal

Jardin
du
Carrousel

Oratoire
du Louvre

125 m

Seine

Musée du Louvre

Pei Pyramid

❺ ALLÉNO PARIS AT PAVILLON LEDOYEN

8 avenue Dutuit, carré des Champs-Élysées, 75008
yannick-alleno.com

Three Michelin Stars. The showcase of cutting-edge chef Yannick Alléno, formerly of the Hotel Meurice. Jolting contrasts are his trademark: duck roasted in a sugar crust; avocados 18 months on the tree, served with a *millefeuille* of celery. Seven-course tasting menu: €340.

❻ LE GRAND VÉFOUR

17 rue de Beaujolais, 75001
grand-vefour.com

Two Michelin stars. Probably Paris's oldest surviving restaurant (opened 1784). Opulent 18th-century decor. Noted for desserts, including artichoke ice cream. Set lunch €115. Evenings, think €250 per person. Worth it to dine (in spirit) with Napoleon, Thomas Jefferson, Colette and Jean Cocteau.

❼ L'ATELIER

Hotel du Pont Royal, 5 rue de Montalembert, 75007
atelier-robuchon-saint-germain.com

Two Michelin stars. Chef Joël Robuchon's 12 restaurants worldwide possess collectively 28 Michelin stars, an international record. Signature dishes include cauliflower cream with caviar and potato puree, and caramelized quail stuffed with *foie gras*. Twelve-course tasting menu: €179 per person.

❽ ALAIN DUCASSE AT PLAZA ATHÉNÉE

Hotel Plaza Athénée, 25 avenue Montaigne, 75008
alain-ducasse.com

Three Michelin stars. For the latest addition to his string of restaurants, the redesigned salon of this luxury hotel, Chef Ducasse announced a return to simplicity and nature, signaled by organic ingredients, little or no red meat, and tables without linen. Lobster, turbot, fruits and fresh herbs feature in his three-course lunch for €210 and dinner for €390.

FORGET THE FOOD: EAT THE DECOR

⑨ LASSERRE

*17 avenue Franklin Delano
Roosevelt, 75008*
restaurant-lasserre.com
With its retractable walls and
roof opening to the sky, Lasserre
is a show in itself, even before
one opens the menu. A six-
course tasting menu, including
two desserts, costs €195. Adding
an appropriate wine for each
course brings the total to €350.
However, it's worth ordering *à
la carte* to sample the signature
dish, Pigeon André Malraux.

⑩ LE JULES VERNE

avenue Gustave Eiffel, 75000
lejulesverne-paris.com
Another restaurant of chef Alain
Ducasse, this one is inside the
Eiffel Tower, and named for the
famous science fiction author.
A favorite of writer Guy de
Maupassant, it was the one
place in Paris he couldn't see
the tower. Spectacular views. A
three-course lunch for €105 per
person and a six-course dinner
for €230.

⑪ LAPÉROUSE

*51 quai des Grands Augustins,
75006*
laperouse.com
Eighteenth-century decor and
the bawdy reputation to go with
it. Adequate food, but more
interesting for its private dining
rooms, where crowned heads
could take off their crowns, and
anything else, confident of the
staff's famous discretion. Dinner
for two in a *salle privée* is worth
every penny of €160 per person.

⑫ LA TOUR D'ARGENT

15 quai de la Tournelle, 75005
tourdargent.com
One Michelin star. Called "The
Silver Tower" because it looks
over Paris from a penthouse
on the Seine. Fans of the
animated movie *Ratatouille* will
recognize the location. Famous
for duck in all its aspects.
Menus from €85 to €300.

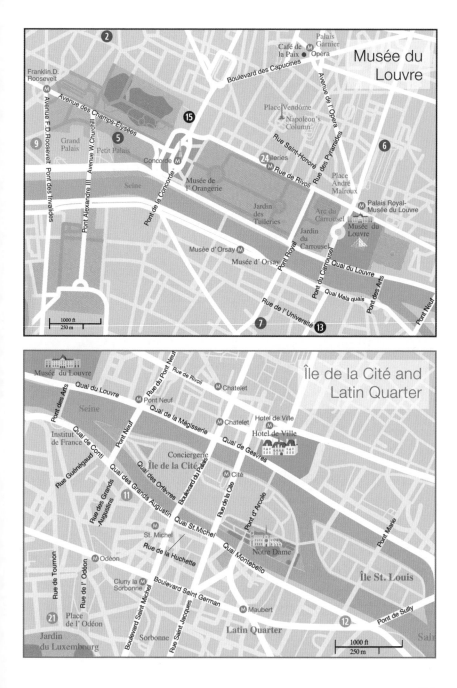

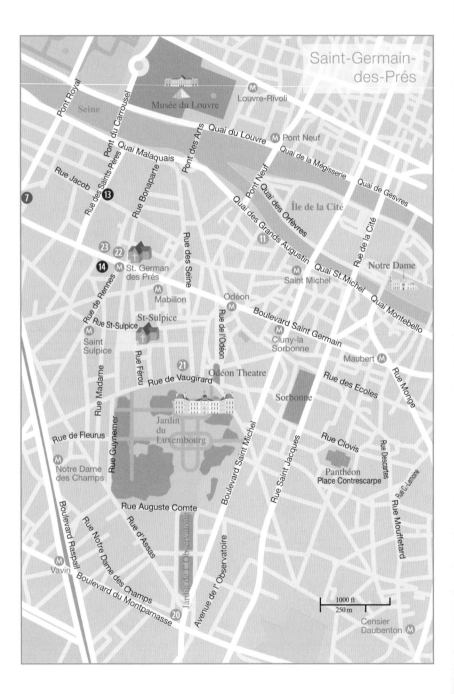

Saint-Germain-
des-Prés

Seine

Pont Royal

Pont du Carrousel

Musée du Louvre

Louvre-Rivoli

Quai Malaquais

Quai du Louvre

Pont Neuf

Quai de la Mégisserie

Rue Jacob

Rue des Saints-Pères

Pont des Arts

Quai de Gesvres

Rue Bonaparte

Pont Neuf

Quai des Orfèvres

Île de la Cité

Rue de la Cité

7

13

Rue des Seine

Quai des Grands Augustin

11

Notre Dame

Quai Montebello

23 **22**

14 St. German
des Prés

Quai St-Michel

Saint Michel

Mabillon

Odéon

Boulevard Saint Germain

Rue de Rennes

St-Sulpice

Rue St-Sulpice

Rue de l'Odéon

Cluny-la
Sorbonne

Saint
Sulpice

Rue Férou

Maubert

Rue Monge

21

Odéon Theatre

Rue des Ecoles

Rue de Vaugirard

Sorbonne

Rue Madame

Jardin
du
Luxembourg

Boulevard Saint Michel

Rue Saint Jacques

Rue Clovis

Rue Descartes

Rue de Fleurus

Rue Guynemer

Panthéon
Place Contrescarpe

Notre Dame
des Champs

Rue C. Lemoine

Rue d'Assas

Rue Auguste Comte

Boulevard Raspail

Rue Notre Dame des Champs

Jardin de l'Observatoire

Avenue de l'Observatoire

Rue Mouffetard

Vavin

Boulevard du Montparnasse

20

1000 ft
250 m

Censier
Daubenton

"X" ATE HERE

⓭ LE COMPTOIR DES SAINTS-PÈRES (formerly MICHAUD)

29 rue des Saints-Pères, 75006.
These days a simple café but
formerly Michaud, famed for
pheasant with potato straws and
woodcock singed with brandy.
Hemingway wrote of James
Joyce, "The report is that he and
all his family are starving, but
you can find the whole Celtic
crew of them in Michaud."
In its toilets, Scott Fitzgerald
once displayed his genitals
to Hemingway, the incident
described in *A Moveable Feast.*

⓮ BRASSERIE LIPP

*151 boulevard St.-Germain,
75006*
brasserielipp.fr
Former brewery/café that
retains its 19th-century decor
and menu. Ernest Hemingway
liked its *cervelas* sausage on cold
boiled potatoes. Also worth
sampling: Alsacian *choucroute*:
sauerkraut made with white
wine and garnished with
sausages and salt pork. Another
obscure delicacy—vintage
canned sardines.

⓯ MAXIM'S

3 rue Royale, 75008
maxims-de-paris.com
Notorious as the *belle époque*'s
prime pickup spot, Maxim's was
celebrated by Proust, Feydeau,
Cocteau, Lehár and Colette,
and patronized by Edward VII,
Dietrich, Garbo, Callas and
Bardot. Not recently, however.
Even without a high-priced
tasting menu, dinner *à la
carte*, with its €50 entrées and
€100 plats, not to mention
the relentlessly promoted
champagne, could run to
€300 or more. Cheaper and
more illuminating to visit the
upstairs museum of *art nouveau*,
recreated under the direction of
Maxim's owner, couturier Pierre
Cardin.

See also CAFÉS.

CAFÉS

The post-World War II decision to serve food in cafés sounded the death
knell for these institutions, crucial to the cultural life of the French

nation. Writers who used their local café as study, office and workroom were pushed out late morning as tables were set for the lunch trade.

⑯ LA COUPOLE

102 boulevard du Montparnasse, 75014. lacoupole-paris.com
Largest and most modern of the great Montparnasse cafés, the Coupole, opened in 1927, combined café, restaurant, cocktail bar and basement dance hall: everything tourists required. Notable for painted columns and floor tiles, both original.

⑰ LE DÔME

108 boulevard du Montparnasse, 75014. restaurant-ledome.com
Favorite hangout of expatriate Americans, including Ernest Hemingway, Henry Miller, etc. A client wrote in 1929, "My dear, at first I was uncertain whether the Dôme was a place or a state of mind or a disease. It is all three!"

⑱ LE SELECT

99 boulevard du Montparnasse, 75006. leselectmontparnasse.fr
Little changed since its opening in 1923. Hemingway drank here, Hart Crane fought with waiters and James Baldwin wrote *Giovanni's Room.*

⑲ CAFÉ DE LA ROTONDE

105 boulevard du Montparnasse, 75006. rotondemontparnasse.com
Meeting place of Hispanic expatriates: Picasso, Gris, Miró. One-time haunt of Amedeo Modigliani.

⑳ CLOSERIE DES LILAS

171 boulevard du Montparnasse, 75006.closeriedeslilas.fr
Venerable hangout of French literary lions. Hemingway wrote in its lilac-shaded café.

㉑ CAFÉ TOURNON

18 rue de Tournon, 75006.
Post-World War II meeting place of African-American expatriates: Richard Wright, Chester Himes, James Baldwin; later of "little magazine" community: George Plimpton, *Paris Review,* etc.

㉒ LES DEUX MAGOTS

6 place Saint-Germain-des-Prés, 75006. lesdeuxmagots.fr
Best-known Paris literary café, named for the Chinese merchants or *megots* perched overhead on the central support column. Expensive but atmospheric.

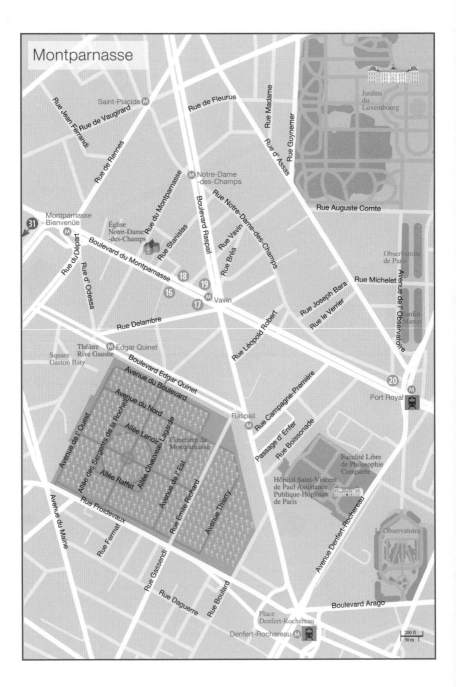

Montparnasse

Rue Jean Ferrandi
Saint-Placide Ⓜ
Rue de Vaugirard
Rue de Fleurus
Rue Madame
Rue Guynemer
Jardins
du
Luxembourg
Rue de Remmes
Rue d' Assas
Rue de Fleurus
Ⓜ Notre-Dame
-des-Champs
Rue Notre-Dame-des-Champs
Rue Auguste Comte
Montparnasse
Bienvenüe
③①
Ⓜ
Rue du Départ
Rue d' Odessa
Boulevard du Montparnasse
Église
Notre-Dame
-des-Champs
Rue du Montparnasse
Boulevard Raspail
Rue Stanislas
Rue Vavin
Rue Bréa
Observatoire
de Paris
Rue Michelet
Avenue de l' Observatoire
⑱
⑯
⑲
⑰
Ⓜ Vavin
Rue Joseph Bara
Rue le Verrier
Jardin
Marco
Rue Delambre
Rue Léopold Robert
Théâtre
Rive Gaushe
Ⓜ Edgar Quinet
Square
Gaston Baty
Boulevard Edgar Quinet
Avenue du Boulevard
Avenue du Nord
Avenue de l' Ouest
Allée des Sergents de la Rochelle
Allée Lenoir Lagarde
Allée Raffet
Allée Chauveau Lagarde
Avenue de l' Est
Cimetière du
Montparnasse
Raspail
Ⓜ Rue Campagne-Première
Passage d' Enfer
Rue Boissonade
⑳
Port Royal 🚉
Faculté Libre
de Philosophie
Comparée
Avenue du Maine
Rue Froidevaux
Rue Fermat
Rue Gassendi
Rue Émile Richard
Avenue Thierry
Hôpital Saint-Vincent
de Paul Assistance
Publique-Hôpitaux
de Paris
Avenue Denfert-Rochereau
L' Observatoire
Rue Daguerre
Rue Boulard
Place
Denfert-Rochereau
Boulevard Arago
Denfert-Rochereau Ⓜ 🚉
200 ft
50 m

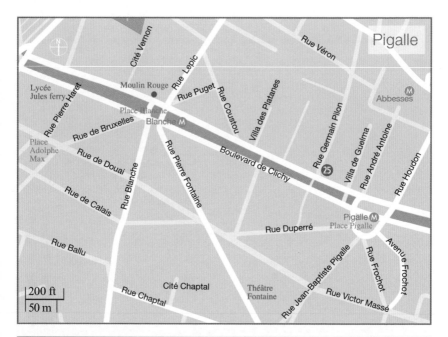

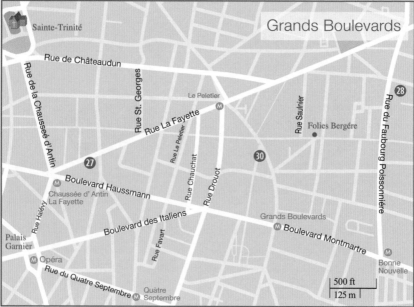

㉓ CAFÉ DE FLORE

172 boulevard Saint-Germain, 75006. cafedeflore.fr

Headquarters of post-World War II Existential movement. Regulars were Jean-Paul Sartre, Simone de Beauvoir, Albert Camus, Juliette Greco.

㉔ ANGELINA

226 rue de Rivoli, 75001 angelina-paris.fr

Famous for patisserie; afternoon tea, coffee or hot chocolate so thick it barely pours. Marcel Proust was a customer.

TRIP-ADVISER TOP TEN

The following were chosen by users of the website TripAdviser as the best Paris restaurants of 2016.

㉕ LES APÔTRES DE PIGALLE

2 rue Germain-Pilon, 75018

Tiny, lively tapas/Hispanic resto in busy Moulin Rouge district.

㉖ IL GRANO

212b boulevard Pereire, 75017 restaurantilgrano.paris

Italian street food, specializing in *pinsa* flatbread.

㉗ MIDI 12

12 rue la Fayette, 75009 http://midi12.lafourchette.rest

Buckwheat pancakes, savory and sweet. Good for a quick lunch between bouts of shopping in Galeries Lafayette and Printemps.

㉘ BISTRO PARADIS

55 rue de Paradis, 75010 bistroparadis.fr

Tiny family resto, attentive service, close to Opera.

EPICURE (See above, under *IF MONEY IS NO OBJECT …*)

㉙ PARIS PICNIC

16 rue Notre Dame de Nazareth, 75003. parispicnic.com

A novel idea: a catered picnic. Cold cuts, cheese, fruit, salad and wine delivered to you near a suitable park: Eiffel Tower, Luxembourg Gardens, etc. Utensils and blanket provided. Professional photographer optional.

③⓪ LOCO

31b rue du Faubourg Montmartre, 75009.

locolerestaurant.com

Steak in all its forms, including super-tender Wagyu beef.

③① LE CLOS Y

27 avenue du Maine, 75015.

leclosy.com

Japanese/French fusion.

LE CINQ. (See above, under *IF MONEY IS NO OBJECT*)

③② IL ÉTAIT UN SQUARE

54 rue Corvisart, 75013.

iletaitunsquare.com

Superior burgers and raw-beef steak tartare.

BON APPÉTIT!

INDEX

CREDITS

Cover: Photo by Helen Cathcart; Page 4: Young Girl Holding French Baguette, c. 1950, photo by Gamma-Keystone via Getty Images; Page 13: Les Cinq Sens, Collection of John Baxter; Page 18: The Son of Man, © René Magritte, Artists Rights Society (ARS), New York 2017; Page 21: 15th-century illumination of a hunting scene, Collection of John Baxter; Page 24: La Double Chasse, Collection of John Baxter; Page 31: Postcard of girl with calf's head, Collection of John Baxter; Page 69: The Glutton, or Big Birds Fly Slowly, Collection of John Baxter; Page 73: Peeling a pear, Collection of John Baxter; Page 78: Women picking figs, Collection of John Baxter; Page 86: The champagne cave of Épernay, © André Galland, Artists Rights Society (ARS), New York 2017; Page 89: Cheese pavilion at Les Halles, photo by ND/ Roger Viollet/Getty Images; Page 93: Goat's milk and cheese seller, photo by Gamma-Keystone via Getty Images; Page 99: Le No. 113, Palais-Royal, Collection of John Baxter; Page 105: Bouillon restaurant, Collection of John Baxter; Page 107: Cooking in a pot, Collection of John Baxter; Page 113: French soldiers cooking chicken for Napoleon, photo by Stefano Bianchetti/Corbis via Getty Images; Page 117: The Plumb-pudding, Collection of John Baxter; Page 128: Paul Verlaine, photo by The Print Collector/ Print Collector/Getty Images; Page 143: Henri Matisse in the Chapel of the Rosary, photo by Dmitri Kessel/The LIFE Images Collection/Getty Images; Page 149: Paolo Montarsolo, photo by Erich Auerbach/Hulton Archive/Getty Images; Page 152: Tournedos Rossini, Collection of John Baxter; Page 157: Franco-Prussian War, photo by Art Media/ Print Collector/Getty Images; Page 165: Voisin's menu, photo by Georges Gobet/ AFP/Getty Images; Page 179: Autumnal Cannibalism, © Salvador Dalí, Fundació Gala-Salvador Dalí, Artists Rights Society (ARS), New York 2017; Page 182: Aimez-vous les femmes?, Collection of John Baxter; Page 187: Jean-Paul Sartre and Simone de Beauvoir, photo by David E. Scherman/The LIFE Picture Collection/Getty Images; Page 195: Josephine Baker, photo by George Hoyningen-Huene/Condé Nast via Getty Images; Page 203: Dalí and Gala, photo by Bettmann/Getty Images; Page 205: The Persistence of Memory, © Salvador Dalí, Fundació Gala-Salvador Dalí, Artists Rights Society (ARS), New York 2017; Page 211: German soldiers at Restaurant à La Mère Catherine, photo by Art Media/Print Collector/Getty Images; Page 214: Partie Surprise, Collection of John Baxter; Page 237: Salon du Chocolat, photo by Richard Bord/Getty Images; Page 238: The dish by chef Alan Ducasse, Photo by Benjamin Auger/Paris Match via Getty Images; Page 242: At Le Grand Défour, photo by Pierre Suu/ Stringer/Getty Images

ABOUT MUSEYON

Named after the Mouseion, the ancient library of Alexandria, Museyon is a New York City-based independent publisher that explores cultural obsessions such as art, history and travel. Expertly curated and carefully researched, Museyon books offer rich entertainment, with fascinating anecdotes, beautiful images and quality information.

Publisher: Akira Chiba
Editor: Janice Battiste
Proofing Editor: Francis Lewis
Cover Designer: José Antonio Contreras

ACCLAIMED BOOKS BY JOHN BAXTER

CHRONICLES OF OLD PARIS
Exploring the Historic City of Light
(ISBN 9780984633425, 288 pages, full color)

Discover one of the world's most fascinating and beautiful cities through 30 dramatic true stories spanning the rich history of Paris. Essays explore major historic events, from the martyrdom of Saint Denis near today's Abbesses Métro station to the epic romances of Héloïse and Abelard, Joséphine and Napoléon, and George Sand and Frédéric Chopin.

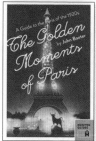

THE GOLDEN MOMENTS OF PARIS
A Guide to the Paris of the 1920s
(ISBN 9780984633470, 288 pages, full color)

Learn about Gertrude Stein and her famous writers' salon, Salvador Dalí and the Surrealists, the birth of Chanel No. 5, and the antics of Ernest Hemingway, F. Scott Fitzgerald and the "lost generation." Then, see what their haunts look like today by following along on the guided walking tours of Paris' historic neighborhoods.

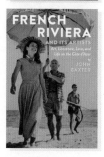

FRENCH RIVIERA AND ITS ARTISTS
Art, Literature, Love, and Life on the Côte d'Azur
(ISBN 9781940842059, 280 pages, full color)

In 21 vivid chapters filled with little-known facts and anecdotes, author John Baxter weaves fascinating true stories about the iconic figures indelibly linked to the South of France—artist Henri Matisse, who lived in Nice for much of his life; F. Scott Fitzgerald, whose Riviera hosts inspired his controversial *Tender Is the Night*; Coco Chanel, who made the Saint-Tropez tan an international fashion statement; and many more.

"Evokes a strong sense of place"
　　　　　—The New York Times

"Packs a good bit of history into one handy source"
　　　　　　　　—Publishers Weekly

"Lovely, gorgeous and intelligent"
　　　　　—Chicago Tribune

"This little gem is as much fun for the armchair traveler
as it is for the tourist"　　　　*—Library Journal*

ABOUT THE AUTHOR

John Baxter is an Australian-born writer, journalist and filmmaker; he has called Paris home since 1989. He is the author of numerous books, including the autobiographical *The Most Beautiful Walk in the World: A Pedestrian in Paris, Chronicles of Old Paris: Exploring The Historic City of Light* and *The Golden Moments of Paris: A Guide to the Paris of the 1920s.*